FINDING
FREEDOM

FINDING
FREEDOM

The Untold Story of
Joshua Glover, Runaway Slave

RUBY WEST JACKSON

WALTER T. MCDONALD

WISCONSIN HISTORICAL SOCIETY PRESS

Published by the Wisconsin Historical Society Press

www.wisconsinhistory.org

Photographs identified with PH, WHi, or WHS are from the Society's collections; address inquiries about such photos to the Visual Materials Archivist at the above address.

Publications of the Wisconsin Historical Society Press are available at quantity discounts for promotions, fund raising, and educational use. Write to the above address for more information.

Printed in the United States of America
Cover design by Nancy Warnecke, Moonlit Ink
Text design by Dedicated Business Solutions

11 10 09 08 07   1 2 3 4 5

Library of Congress Cataloging-in-Publication Data

Jackson, Ruby West.
  Finding freedom : the untold story of Joshua Glover, runaway slave / Ruby West Jackson and Walter T. McDonald.
    p. cm.
  Includes bibliographical references and index.
  ISBN-13: 978-0-87020-382-4 (hardcover : alk. paper) 1. Glover, Joshua. 2. Fugitive slaves—United States—Biography. 3. Fugitive slaves—Wisconsin—Biography. 4. Glover, Joshua—Friends and associates. 5. Underground railroad—Wisconsin. 6. Antislavery movements—Wisconsin—History—19th century. 7. African Americans—Ontario—Biography. 8. Slaves—Missouri—Saint Louis—Biography. 9. Racine (Wis.)—Biography. 10. Etobicoke (Ont.)—Biography. I. McDonald, Walter T. II. Title.
  E450.G58J33 2008
  973.7'115092—dc22
  [B]
                                                              2006028144

Front cover: Illustration from the July 1837 *Anti-slavery record*. WHS library E449 A6238.

To all those who have had to flee, often leaving family and friends, because they could not abide the strictures of slavery; to the memory of the many thousands who found freedom in Mexico, in the Caribbean, among various Indian nations, and in Canada; to the memory of all who assisted them; and to the citizens and the Commonwealth of Canada who provided refuge to our oppressed and disaffected from the time of the American Revolution, through the Vietnam War, to the rescue of our hostages in Iran, this book is dedicated.

Joshua fit the battle of Jericho, Jericho, Jericho
Joshua fit the battle of Jericho and the walls come tumblin' down
— Anonymous American Spiritual

Contents

Acknowledgments

No book is the result exclusively of the efforts of those whose names are on the title page. Without the expertise, gracious cooperation, and resourcefulness of dozens of people in two countries, five states, and fifteen cities and towns, this book would not exist. Some we never came to know by name; others we eventually came to call friends.

In Wisconsin, Richard Ammann, Ph.D., archivist of the Racine Heritage Museum, in addition to finding information we requested, called several times to tell us of new material he had unearthed or recently acquired.

John Buenker, Ph.D., professor emeritus of history at the University of Wisconsin–Parkside, critically read our manuscript and corrected some errors. In addition, we thank our other readers: Leslie Lindenauer, Ph.D., of Hartford College for Women; Amanda Todd, Public Information Office, Wisconsin Supreme Court; Glynette Tilley Turner, author of a number of books on the Underground Railroad (UGRR); Betty Stinson, friend and educational and curriculum specialist with Racine Unified School District; Ethel Swonigan, friend and avid reader of the genre; and Genevieve McBride, professor of women's studies at the University of Wisconsin–Milwaukee, who was also instrumental in directing our publisher's attention to our manuscript.

Margo Drummond, a Racine Cemetery commissioner, provided helpful information on nineteenth-century residents. Mary Josten generously gave us the research files of her late husband, local attorney Roy Josten, who was gathering material for a book on the legal implications of the Glover case.

Gerald L. Karwoski, owner of Oak Clearings Museum and Library, provided copies of valuable early histories. Russell Schwartz

Jr., an excellent cartographer, created the maps that illustrate Joshua Glover's travels on the UGRR. The staff of the reference desk at the Racine Public Library was helpful in locating obscure sources and in securing other material through interlibrary loans.

In Rochester, Wisconsin, Ed and Wendy Ela gave freely of their time in providing information about their ancestor, who assisted Glover, and they arranged for one of us to talk to the Rochester Historical Society about our research needs. Don Vande Sand, archivist and historian at the Burlington Historical Museum, in addition to spending hours locating material on former residents of the area who had been instrumental in helping Glover, was also available for phone consultation.

In Milwaukee, the staffs of the Milwaukee Historical Society's research library and of the Humanities Department of Milwaukee Public Library were able to provide information on figures linked to Glover and on Racine's maritime connection to the UGRR. Albert Muchka, associate curator and American History Collection manager of the Milwaukee Public Museum, provided information on Milwaukee's black pioneers and on an important protest meeting that took place following passage of the Fugitive Slave Act in 1850.

Enough cannot be said about the skills of Lori Bessler, microforms librarian of the Wisconsin Historical Society in Madison, who is always ready to go that extra yard for people engaged in research. In addition, Holly Fleming of Webster House Museum of Walworth County; Eric Vanden Heuvel, archivist of Waukesha County Historical Society and Museum; and Cindy Nelson, archivist of Kenosha Historical Museum, provided freely their time and expertise.

In Chicago, Glenn Longacre, archivist with the Midwest Branch of the National Archives and Research Administration, found for us invaluable material on the efforts of Booth's and Garland's attorneys to prevail against each other, even going so far as to locate and copy for us the original document in which President James Buchanan remitted Booth's sentence.

In Alton, Illinois, Eric Robinson, who, in addition to being a historian, a tour operator, and a faculty member of Lewis and Clark Community College, is also one of the hereditary caretakers of the burial site of abolitionist Elijah Lovejoy. He provided information about important UGRR connections between St. Louis and Alton.

In St. Louis, the staff of the Missouri Historical Society pointed us to Garland's fugitive slave notice and other material related to him. Jim Vincent, local black history and UGRR specialist, opened doors for us that would have been exceedingly difficult to pry open on our own and guided us through contemporary St. Louis so we could attempt to locate the site of Garland's farm. Melvina Conley, archivist of the Twenty-second Judicial Circuit of Missouri, provided one of the great finds of our search. Without her assistance, we would likely never have discovered Garland's other job. In Jefferson City, Missouri, Alice Henson, a genealogist, supplied material on Garland's agricultural yields and his various residences over a period of more than thirty years.

In Lynchburg, Virginia, Louis Hobgood Averett of Jones Memorial Library provided material on Garland family genealogy, family land holdings in the area, and various property and slave transactions. The staff at Point of Honor, a local museum of early American history, provided a slide of their fine oil painting of Garland as well as family material.

In the borough of Etobicoke, in Ontario, Canada, Randall Reid, historian at Montgomery's Inn, provided a briefing on this former home of Glover's employer, which is now a "living museum." Additionally, the staff provided access to many important documents. The staffs of the Archives of Ontario and of the Baldwin Room of Toronto's Metropolitan Reference Library gave us access to voluminous Montgomery material and facilitated acquisition of copies of important documents related to Glover.

Hilary Dawson of Toronto, a historian and chronicler of the lives of runaway slaves living in the area, was a docent at Montgomery's Inn when we first met her. She was also a provider of research materials on Glover and his life in Canada. Her prodigious efforts and her ability to unearth events concerning Glover will be detailed more fully elsewhere.

In addition to providing information to us, there were others who provided emotional support during our years of effort: Barbara Tagger, southeast regional coordinator of the Underground

Railroad Network to Freedom, a division of the National Park Service; Hermetta Williams, former administrator, Wisconsin Bureau of Minority Business; and H. Nicholas Mueller, former director, Wisconsin Historical Society.

George Gonis, in addition to reading the manuscript and suggesting other readers to us, was of great assistance in our search for a publisher and was tireless in his promotion of our efforts.

To Stephen Schenkenberg, our editor, for his encouragement and patience in guiding our original manuscript to its final form, our sincere appreciation.

Finally, our thanks to the nearby and far-flung children of our respective families, with a special nod of appreciation to Jacquelyn Jackson for her efforts, which included the reading of the manuscript.

Our apologies to any whose names were inadvertently omitted. We are, of course, solely responsible for the use we made of materials provided and for any errors that may have resulted.

1

A Slave in St. Louis

It was New Year's Day, 1850. Joshua stood among the other men, women, and children who were to be offered for sale from the steps of the St. Louis Courthouse at this auction of human property.[1] The cold wind blowing off the nearby Mississippi River chilled their ill-clad bodies. They waited their turn to be poked, prodded, and examined by the auctioneer and prospective buyers.

A large number of St. Louis slave owners and onlookers surrounded the east side of the brick building where the annual New Year's auction would shortly begin. There was a somewhat festive air as the owners contemplated improvement in their fortunes in the coming year through the purchases and hires they would make that day. This ritual was taking place at the same time throughout many cities of the South and the border states. For many of these owners, some of whom had moved from the Lower South to Missouri to establish slavery there, it was more than a business transaction. It was also an occasion to revel in the pride of ownership their position brought them.

Of the two groups assembled, the one there by choice was marked by uniformly paler skin as well as brighter, newer, and more fashionable clothes. Some first-time buyers even wore clothing more elegant than they could easily afford, thereby celebrating their prestigious entry into the slaveholding classes. The busy hum of their conversation was like that of an orchestra tuning up for a favorite piece. The skins of those present involuntarily were of shades from the ebony, umber, ocher, and amber sections of the palette, with some who appeared more white than black or brown.

1

Their coarse and worn clothing was composed in part of the castoffs of the other group.

For those about to be sold, it was the most dreadful of days, filled with deep sorrow and fear to the point of terror, as they contemplated the separation from families that was imminent for some—husbands and wives pulled from each other's embrace while begging and pleading not to be split up, infants snatched from their mothers' breasts, milk still dripping from their lips, milk that would soon be used to nurse and nourish their new masters' infants. So distressing were such situations that, in some instances, mothers ended their children's lives as well as their own rather than surrender to separation. The scene was one of much weeping and distress. But even in their grief, they had to mask the full intensity of their feelings. To be too vocal in their expression could bring swift blows from the keepers, who had brought their charges from the nearby "nigger pens," where some had been confined for up to several days prior to the imminent sale.[2]

Such pens were actually private jails in which slaves, intended for sale or hire, could be kept and examined prior to the sale. One of the more prominent traders, Bernard Lynch, had for many years a succession of pens in the vicinity of the courthouse. In his advertisements he assured the public that he had "a good yard for their accommodation and comfortable quarters under secure fastenings."[3] A visiting clergyman once had the opportunity to tour one of Lynch's pens. Lynch led the cleric to the jail's entrance, drew out a great iron key, inserted it in the lock, turned back the bolt, and, swinging open the door, expressed regret that his stock was so small. He then locked the door, remaining outside while his visitor examined the interior. The room had one small window, located near the ceiling. The floor was bare earth, and the furniture consisted of three wooden benches without backs. There were seven slaves within the room, and both sexes were herded together without any arrangement for privacy. During the inspection, one woman of about forty tearfully begged the visitor to buy her, repeatedly promising to be faithful and good.[4]

In addition to operating one of the largest slave dealerships in St. Louis, Lynch was also a clever businessman when it came to controlling his inventory. On tax-assessment day in 1852, 1857, and 1860, he was careful not to be holding a sale, and he was taxed on only three, three, and four slaves, respectively.[5] This ploy resulted in lower taxes than would have been assessed if he had the greater number that was usually in residence immediately preceding a sale.

The hiring of slaves usually took place before the outright sales. This form of restricted slave trading represented a less publicized but increasingly profitable aspect of slave dealing. Among the many reasons for the existence of this practice was the opportunity to have the services of one or more slaves at a lower cost than ownership while still affording membership in the elite group of slaveholders. It was also a method among the land-poor gentry of managing their increasing indebtedness.[6]

One observer of slave trading and hiring in Virginia in the 1850s, Joseph Holt Ingraham of Mississippi, commented that slaves were raised "more as a marketable and money-returning commodity than for their productive labor."[7] Using probate records of values of slaves and rental fees paid for hiring them, one investigator estimated that hiring male slaves rather than purchasing them produced a rate of return equal to about 14 percent of the value of the slave, quite a healthy profit considering that there was no responsibility by the owner for providing food, shelter, and clothing.[8]

Slaves were, of course, also sold outright. Some of these were purchased for local use, and others were bought for use in plantations farther south. It was not an uncommon sight to see coffles of chained slaves being led from the courthouse to the river for their journey south. One former slave, who was sold from the east side of the courthouse in 1847, three years before Joshua stood on that same spot, later reported, "I have seen a line of slaves, two abreast, two squares long, marching to the boats to be shipped South. Each negro was handcuffed and they were chained together just like criminals."[9]

On that New Year's Day in 1850, David McCullough, the marshal of St. Louis, stood off to the side of the courthouse entrance, strategically placed so he could observe both the assembled buyers and the slaves. He was there to assure that the sale was conducted in an orderly fashion and that the slaves caused no trouble to their present or prospective owners.[10]

This oil painting shows the last slave sale from the steps of St. Louis Courthouse, ten years after Joshua was sold from that spot to Benammi S. Garland.

Among those owners was one fashionably dressed man whose appearance would be noted in any crowd. He had a slight build, a high forehead, and compelling green eyes widely set on either side of a long, slender nose, which was perched above a wide mouth with a very full lower lip; a slightly dimpled chin completed the picture of a handsome young aristocrat. Benammi Stone Garland, originally from Lynchburg, Virginia, was in his early forties and had lived in St. Louis for more than ten years. He had come to town that day to make a purchase.[11]

Throughout the slaveholding states, the forms of slave sales varied only in the number of slaves being auctioned and in the degrees of indignities levied against the subjects. As the slaves were offered for inspection, the auctioneer or his assistants roughly stripped them of their clothes or required them to disrobe themselves so their bodies might be examined for signs of ill health. Backs were checked for whip marks so it could be determined if a slave was a "bad nigger," one who had been punished frequently and was therefore thought to be rebellious. (The assumption was much less likely to be made that he was being sold by a bad master.) Often the slave's mouth was pried open to determine both whether he had all his teeth and whether he was a "blue gum nigger." There was a superstition that one had to avoid being bitten by a slave with such coloration because such a bite was more deadly than that of a rattlesnake.[12]

As if being sold were not indignity enough, slaves were often required to contribute to a successful sale by enthusiastically declaiming their skills and virtues to the prospective buyers. For the slave this was a hazardous aspect of the sale. Refusal to speak might result in a beating on the spot. If the slave exaggerated his skills to avoid punishment, he might be punished later when his new owner discovered that he had been misled.

When Joshua was stripped, the crowd could see that there were no marks on his back. When told to describe his skills, he would have been honestly able to talk about both his strength and his stamina in being able to work long hours. He could talk about being able to split more rails faster and straighter than most. He could detail his ability to dig numerous postholes and tell how fast he could chop and stack cordwood. Finally, he could testify to his skill in wielding a scythe to mow a field.[13] Convinced that he would be a good buy, as well as a "good boy," Garland ended the bidding with his purchase of Joshua and arranged for Joshua to be transported to his farm located near the Prairie House about four miles west of the city by way of the St. Charles Plank Road.[14]

As he boarded the agent's wagon with other slaves who were being transported to their new owners following the recent sale, Joshua was likely very aware that his purchase by Garland might have spared him the fate of many who had been sold south.[15] As he was driven away, he would have been able to see the coffles of slaves being led through the streets to the waterfront. There they would be herded onto boats bound for farms and plantations farther south, a reenactment of a tradition that had begun in the interior of West Africa more than two hundred years before, when traders brought the first slaves to embarkation points on the ocean for what would eventually be called "the Middle Passage" to the colonies that would become the United States of America.[16]

Garland may have heard little or nothing of Joshua before the purchase, except for Joshua's strength and skills as a worker. Owners of human property had relatively little knowledge about the thoughts, feelings, and character of their chattel. To trouble themselves about such details would indicate that they believed their property had the same human feelings they possessed. Such sentiments would have been an impediment to the efficient management of their source of labor. It might also have made them feel guilty about the treatment slaves received at their hands, an emotion that would interfere with the effort to obtain maximum effort with minimum cost.

Joshua, on the other hand, would have certainly known many things about Garland. Because he had probably lived in the area for some time, he would have already heard of "Massa" Garland. He might have known that Garland's wife's name was Isabelle and that she was also called Belle. He would have known that she was younger than her husband, although he might not have guessed the difference to be ten years. He would have known that the family had three young boys, and he would learn very quickly to call them "young Massas Joseph, Adison, and Ben." Some of this information he would have overheard by paying close attention to everything the white people around him said, while pretending to be minding his own business. The rest he would have learned from other slaves he would encounter in his daily life, including during religious services that some slaves were permitted to attend. Not all slaves were allowed to go to church; although owners were eager to have their slaves hear and absorb the lessons of clergymen preaching the biblical exhortation "Servants, obey thy masters," they were fearful that such occasions would also provide a venue for slaves to share information that could eventually lead to their escape.

It would be critical for Joshua to learn much more about Garland to ensure that his life with him would be as free from hazard as he could make it. This knowledge would be the only power Joshua possessed to improve life in slavery. He had to know about the moods of the owner and his wife, which of the children to be wary of, what pleased and displeased various members of the family, and any other information he could glean that would protect him from harm. Most of all, he had to be appropriately subservient and avoid appearing to have more knowledge than his owner about anything. Maintaining this posture assisted the owner in perpetuating the fiction that his chattel was lazy, ignorant, and incapable of being taught by any means other than the application of force. Failing to observe this fiction could result in a charge of being "uppity" or perhaps even a beating. This is one reason why the replies of slaves to their masters' questions were often outright lies, suggesting that they were satisfied with their lives in slavery. The prevalence of this was noted in 1864, when an interviewer, talking to escaped slaves in Canada, observed, "The negro, like other men, naturally desires to live in the light of truth; but he hides in the shadow of falsehood, more or less deeply, according as his safety or welfare seems to require it. Other things equal, the freer a people, the more truthful; and only the perfectly free and fearless are perfectly truthful."[17]

To limit slaves' ability to live in the light of such truths, the Missouri legislature and the St. Louis authorities passed various laws and ordinances regulating slaves. Among these were the ability to assemble at a public mill "with leave," except at night or on Sunday. In addition, slaves could go to church only by written consent. In 1847, every religious assembly of Negroes or mulattos was required, if the preacher was a Negro, to have some official present "in order to prevent all seditious speeches and disorderly and unlawful conduct of any kind." An ordinance of 1835 punished a slave with five to fifteen lashes for being at a religious or other meeting without permission later than nine o'clock at night from October to March, or after ten o'clock the other six months of the year.[18] Those proscriptions notwithstanding, many slaves still found ingenious ways of communicating with one another, including using well-known coded spirituals. Most slave owners would have been amazed if they knew how much information their slaves truly had, not only about them, but about every owner within the area ever likely to have an effect on them, whether because of being owned by them, being hired out to them, or simply having delivered something from one owner to another. As the gathering of military intelligence is essential to victory in war, so was it also essential in the not-yet-openly declared war of slavery versus freedom.

Following the sale on the courthouse steps, Joshua likely spent his first evening at Garland's acquainting himself with the other slaves and garnering as much additional information as he could about his new owner before beginning work the next day. Anticipating the winter dawn, Joshua and the other slaves would have awoken in their quarters the next morning while it was still dark to make preparations for a day that would not end until after the sun had set.

Garland had no overseer and would have given orders directly to Joshua. Because he had arrived at the Garland farm in the winter, Joshua's initial duties were not as likely to have occurred in the field but probably involved caring for the animals and repairing and maintaining equipment, as well as clearing land, splitting rails, and cutting wood for fuel. Some of the slaves would have had to muck out the cow barn and stable to provide compost for fertilizer.

Although Garland would eventually call Joshua the foreman of his farm, it is not clear whether that was a fact or a claim made by Garland later to inflate his value for compensation purposes.[19] (Slaves were not the only ones who lied when it suited their purpose.) As he went about the duties assigned by Garland, Joshua familiarized himself with his owner's operation and investigated much of the land and where it led, as time and circumstances permitted.

On his three hundred-acre farm, Garland had two hundred acres under cultivation. From this land in 1850, he harvested 2,000 bushels of corn, 300 of oats, and 150 of potatoes, and he kept a small orchard. His biggest crop by far was the almost two hundred tons of hay produced. He had a dairy herd of twenty-one cows that had to be milked twice a day and an additional ten head of cattle, along with twenty swine. In addition to milking, the slaves were actively involved in making butter, producing more than one thousand pounds one year. Part of the labor on Garland's farm, including transportation around the countryside and into town, was carried out by the ten horses he owned, with the rest being done by his six slaves.[20]

In addition to Joshua, who was about thirty-six years old, there were three other males, ages eighteen, sixteen, and fifteen, and two females, a woman, thirty-six, and a girl, nine. It is likely that the woman was a house slave, doing the cooking, laundering, and similar duties, with the girl helping and looking after Benjamin, who was almost three.[21] Garland estimated the value of his farm at sixty thousand dollars, which did not include the value of the equipment, implements, livestock, or slaves, nor of the commodities and produce.[22] Garland was a very wealthy man.

He also had another source of income, and this one he derived from his own efforts without assistance from his slaves. Had Garland not had those slaves, however, he would not have had the time required to devote to his other enterprise. Beginning in the 1840s, he began purchasing, probably at a discount, notes other men were holding against their debtors when they found themselves in need of cash. He then collected those debts at face value plus accrued interest. When he could not collect a debt, he frequently used the courts to assist him in his efforts. Methodical in the pursuit of that which was owed him, Garland made many trips to court, winning all of his suits in lower courts and then winning also in the court of appeals when challenged there by the defendants.[23]

One of Garland's attempts at collection of a debt owed to him is worthy of recounting because of its relationship to one of the most important cases in the history of slavery in Missouri, as well as the country as a whole. In a document filed in probate court in St. Louis in 1859, Benammi Garland demanded that "on account of services in selling land negroes and personal property and attention t[o Dr]ed Scott and other negroes amounting to one thousand forty dollars and ninety cents . . ." he is still owed a substantial sum of money. Although one of the inkblots on the page partially obscures the first name of the man who may well have been the most famous slave in America, there is no doubt as to his identity, because the suit was filed against Chauvin LeBeau, administrator of the estate of John F. A. Sanford.[24] Sanford was the defendant in the case of *Dred Scott v. Sanford*, which was decided by Chief Justice Roger Taney in 1856 in favor of slaveholders and which also hastened the country into civil war.

The exact date that Garland provided service to Dred Scott's owner is not known, but it was probably while Scott was still owned by Irene Emerson, the widow of Dr. John Emerson, the U.S. Army surgeon who had moved to Illinois and then to Wisconsin Territory, taking Scott with him, thus freeing Scott under both the 1787 Northwest Ordinance and Missouri law. When she planned to move out of the state following her husband's death, she arranged for the St. Louis sheriff to undertake hiring out her slaves and holding the rental fees in escrow until the suit for freedom of Dred and his wife, Harriet, was settled.[25] Garland appears to have been involved in this case at least as early as March 1847, judging from an 1852 jury verdict that awarded him $457.88, which included interest of $100.16 from the earlier date to the date of judgment.[26]

As late as February 1859, Garland was still attempting to collect his account. This relentless approach to recovering that which was owed to him was a trait of Garland's that Joshua would observe and remember long after he had left Missouri.

Garland's farm was only a few miles downstream from the city of Alton, Illinois, a stronghold of abolitionist sentiment and the former home of the abolitionist and newspaper editor Elijah Lovejoy, who had been murdered by proslavery forces in 1837 and whose presses were thrown into the river. Elijah was the brother of Owen Lovejoy, whose home in Princeton, Illinois, was a station on the Underground Railroad (UGRR) on the way to Wisconsin.

On Garland's farm of three hundred acres there were ample places to explore without being seen and many opportunities to estimate the distance to the river. While acting the role of a contented slave, pleased with his kind owner, someone like Joshua could certainly find opportunities to learn from other slaves. There were whispered tales of who had escaped, which methods had been used, what had worked, and what had failed. Although the next version of the Fugitive Slave Law would not be signed into law for more than a year and a half, there was already ample news available about slave owners' concerns over the increasing number of runaways from Missouri. In 1847, the Missouri legislature asked Congress for more effective legislation for the return of slaves, "as the citizens of this State are annually subjected to heavy losses of property, by the escape of their slaves, who pass through the State of Illinois, and finally find a secure place of refuge in Canada."[27] Some years later, a Missouri newspaper editor asked, "When will the abominable practice of man-stealing, practiced by a portion of our northern people, find their operations checkmated and discountenanced by that professedly Christian and law-abiding people?"[28]

Joshua's inability to read these comments would have been no barrier to his learning of them. Although, as a field slave, he had probably never been in Garland's house, an adult slave working inside would have probably passed on what was heard to those who worked in the fields. This is often how slaves learned what their master and his friends were discussing, as well as what they said about punishments meted out to escaping slaves who had been captured.

Slaves' fears of punishment that would follow a failed attempt at escape were partially offset by their knowledge that others had been successful. This optimism prevailed in spite of the lies told by the owners about conditions in Canada. Various slaves had been told that Canada was nine thousand miles away, that it was so cold that when you were cutting grass the thick ice would stop your scythe, that half your labor earnings would go to the Queen, that there were no animals there, and that they didn't raise much at all. Many of the former slaves retold these stories when they were interviewed after their arrival in Canada.[29]

Long before Benammi Garland set foot in Missouri, his father, James Parker Garland knew that the family's fortunes would not continue to prosper if his children remained in Virginia. Due to the overplanting of tobacco, a good bit of the land was being leached of its nutrients. The West was being opened to expansion following the Louisiana Purchase, and the passage of the Missouri Compromise in 1820 enabled that territory to enter the Union as a slave state. All these factors combined to turn his thoughts westward, and he was not the only Southerner to do so.

When the French province of Louisiana was sold to the United States in 1803, slave property in that part of the territory that constituted Missouri was already thought to be guaranteed. Slaveholders became upset when that portion known as the St. Louis District was placed under the government of the Indiana Territory, because slavery was prohibited in that territory. They were eventually successful in their efforts to have slavery maintained in the St. Louis District. They also succeeded in having the slave laws of the new Missouri Territory follow those of the Virginia statutes.[30]

In the 1830s, when James Parker Garland paid for Benammi to take what was possibly a scouting trip to Missouri, he was already aware that many Virginians as well as other Southerners had been heading that way for a number of years. Between 1820, when Missouri was guaranteed the right to enter as a slave state, and 1830, the population of slaves grew from slightly more than ten thousand to a bit more than twenty-five thousand, an increase of a shade more than 150 percent.[31]

Some time after Benammi returned from his journey, probably about the mid-1830s, he and his two brothers, Adison and Alexander, moved to Missouri, taking with them several slaves, who were later willed to them by their maternal grandfather, Benammi Stone.[32] Once there, Garland began to set up the operation that greeted Joshua on the morning of his first day on Garland's farm.

This then is the situation that Joshua entered at the beginning of January 1850 as "a servant for life." As Joshua had been born a slave, so was Garland born a patrician member of the landed gentry, marrying into a similar family. The crossing of their paths in 1850 was in itself no more remarkable than any other similar transaction that took place that year. What took place following their association of slightly more than three years would, however, set in motion a series of events that would have a profound effect on both men and on the country as a whole. It would build some careers and wreck others. It would be a catalyst speeding the formation of the only third party to endure as part of the two-party system. It would result in a Northern state, Wisconsin, attempting to nullify the U.S. Constitution. That state would then condemn South Carolina less than a decade later, when its use of the same device resulted in civil war. Finally, it would lead Joshua to a life of freedom in Canada that would extend almost as long as had his life of bondage.

2

The "Peculiar Institution"

Benammi Garland's home state of Virginia was among the first to define slavery as an institution. In the early days of the colony, it was often unclear whether a worker was indentured or enslaved. In indentured service, an individual entered into a contract to work for another for a specified period of years, following which he was free to leave. An enslaved person was considered to be in that state for life.

That situation was first resolved in Jamestown in the early seventeenth century, when three indentured servants, two white and one black, ran away to Maryland from a farmer for whom they worked. Returned to Jamestown after their capture, all three received thirty lashes. The two white men were sentenced to an additional four years of servitude, one for their employer and three more for the colony. John Punch, the black man, was ordered to "serve his said master or his assigns for the time of his natural Life here or elsewhere." Barely a generation later, in 1662, the Virginia laws stated that children would be born bonded or free, depending on the status of the mother. By 1705, firm slave codes were in place in Virginia, and the practice would survive and prosper throughout the South for the next 160 years.[1]

After the United States emerged victorious from the Revolutionary War with England, the continuance of the institution of slavery was a paramount problem facing the founders. The fledgling nation was not about to risk splintering into two countries over that issue before the union had even been solidified. Both those opposed to slavery and those in favor of it believed there would have to be compromise in this volatile area.

The first of many times that slavery would be subject to compromise arose in the Constitutional Convention of 1787. While there was general agreement that slaves were property and that property could not vote, there was disagreement over whether slaves should be counted in apportioning representation. This desire to avoid a split led the founders to the compromise in the Constitution that stated, "Representatives and direct taxes shall be apportioned among several states . . . according to their respective numbers, which shall be determined by adding to the whole number of free persons . . . three-fifths of all other persons." Thus was created the situation in which a slave became less than a whole person, unable to vote to alter his or her status; but the South, which had the greater number of slaves, was enabled to increase its representation in Congress in defense of the preservation and expansion of slavery.

Though slavery was an entrenched and essential part of the largely agrarian South, slave owners were aware that slaves did not necessarily hold the same point of view about that condition as their masters and might therefore attempt to escape to places where bondage did not exist. Because the Constitution would be able to be amended to bar the importation of slaves after 1808, and because Northern states were gradually outlawing slavery, it was important for slave owners to ensure that efforts to escape to a free state could be legally prohibited and punished. Therefore, Article IV, Section 2 of the Constitution stated that no slave in one state could be discharged from service by escaping to another state and that an escapee must be delivered up to his owner on demand. The Northwest Ordinance of 1787, which established the precedents by which the United States would expand westward by the admission of new states, also stipulated that the policy applied to escape to free territories.

In spite of the contentions of some slaveholders that servitude was the natural state of blacks and that they were happy in their lot, the increasing number of escapes put the lie to this myth. The resulting Fugitive Slave Law of 1793 made it easier to recapture fugitives by requiring only proof of ownership before a magistrate and by forbidding jury trials. These provisions not only made it easier to retrieve a slave but also led to increased kidnappings of free blacks in the North, who were then sold back into slavery. This action, in turn, increased Northern resistance to the enforcement of the act.

Many slaveholders were concerned not only with escapes, but with revolts, there having been a number of them by the midnineteenth century. These fears led to the passage of laws in some Southern states requiring free blacks to carry passes, prohibiting enslaved blacks from congregating in large numbers or from holding church services without supervision, and making it a crime to attempt to learn how to read. These were, of course, rather unnecessary strictures if, as some of their owners claimed, slaves were really happy in their servitude.

Regardless of how the laws were strengthened, escapes continued, sometimes aided by Northern sympathizers. As the country began its westward expansion, the question arose how slavery would fit into the territories petitioning for statehood. In 1820, as Missouri was about to become a state, the recently enacted Missouri Compromise decreed that the number of subsequent slave and free states should always remain equal, so Missouri was admitted as a slave state and Maine, at the same time, as a free state. Those wanting Missouri to be a slave state also inserted a clause in the state constitution barring free Negroes from moving into the state. Because this was contrary to the U.S. Constitution's right to free travel, it was removed. Eventually, slavery was prohibited north of the southern border of Missouri and in the rest of the Louisiana Purchase territory.[2]

Keeping a balance between free and slave states did not reduce the flow of attempted and successful escapes. In the case of Illinois and Missouri, for instance, their proximity provided greater opportunity for slaves to flee their masters. The success of the Southern states in enabling slavery to expand westward with the country encouraged further efforts at spreading slavery; this was met by greater resistance on the part of Northern abolitionists and greater encouragement to slaves to flee northward. While most slaves were unable to read, and those who did could suffer severe punishment if caught doing so, they could still overhear, and they could still communicate the things they learned to other slaves. Because members of the privileged classes often spoke in the presence of their servants as if they did not exist, the servants were given ample opportunities to eavesdrop and learn whose slaves had successfully escaped. Slaves, adopting the pose of the ignorant individuals their owners wished them to be, were thus provided with protective coloration for acquiring information. In such ways they learned of the Underground Railroad and the concerns of their owners that their wealth was draining north.

In yet another effort to stanch the northward flow of its economic lifeblood, the Southern coalition launched its largest damage-control effort to date. The "Great Compromiser," Senator Henry Clay, led the effort that he believed would preserve the Union. The outcome of this effort was the so-called Compromise of 1850, sometimes called the Omnibus Bill. Included in this document was the Fugitive Slave Law of 1850, which, in a few years, would play such important role in the life of Joshua and a number of the citizens of Wisconsin.

The law never referred to runaway slaves by that title, instead calling them "fugitives from labor." It established rules intended to decrease the outflow of slaves and make it easier to return fugitives by punishing more severely those who aided them. Court commissioners were empowered to act as judges and to issue certificates to slave owners, permitting them to claim their property and return home with it. All federal marshals in the states and territories were ordered to carry out the orders of the commissioners. If convicted of willfully failing to do this, a marshal could be fined one thousand dollars. Further, if the slave in custody should escape from the marshal, the marshal would be liable to the owner for the full value of the slave's labor or services. In order to make their task easier, marshals were empowered to form a posse of available citizens to hunt down the escapees and return them to custody. An added provision said that no fugitives might have their testimony admitted in evidence. The only questions to be answered were whether the escapee was a slave and whether service was owed to the person making the claim. Any person harboring, aiding, or abetting a fugitive was subject to a fine of one thousand dollars and imprisonment for up to six months.

To increase the odds that a slave would be returned to servitude, the law decreed that a commissioner determining that insufficient proof existed to return a slave to a petitioner would be paid five dollars. If he issued a certificate authorizing the return of the slave, he would be paid ten dollars. While a charitable interpretation might assume that the greater effort involved in determining that one was a fugitive from service merited greater remuneration, it cannot have escaped the attention of commissioners that issuing a certificate would double one's income from this enterprise.

From 1787 to 1850, as each effort at compromise was hammered into law, so were the rails of the UGRR forged more strongly to bear the increased load of the freight traveling north. Of the many forces tearing at the fabric of the Southern way of life, the continued reliance on manual labor, fostered by the presence of a permanently indentured workforce, probably had more to do with the eventual demise of slavery than did the UGRR. There is little doubt however, that the UGRR was a marvelous propaganda machine. It was a form of largely nonviolent active resistance that proved false every myth constructed by slaveholders that blacks were ignorant, unorganized, and unskilled and could do nothing without the guidance of white men.

To preserve that myth, it was necessary for the South to blame Northern white agitators for fomenting dissatisfaction among slaves. Though partially true, the encouragement of whites in the North was only one more thing goading slaves to resolve to escape the tyranny of bondage. Still, it was necessary for Southerners to create significant civil and criminal punishments for those who assisted slaves to escape. Above all, it was necessary to imply that Negroes could never escape in such numbers without the help of whites.

In his seminal 1961 book *The Liberty Line: The Legend of the Underground Railroad*, however, Larry Gara argued that escaped slaves began their journey to freedom largely independently, sometimes in small groups and most often with little or no help from white abolitionists. He also maintained that many of the stories regarding the UGRR were more myth than reality, fed by unverified legend and short on facts, with much of the information being supplied by the time-distorted memories of participants, many years after the fact.[3] While this is an important observation, designed to alert readers to the possibility of unreliable accounts, it is important to note that when Gara reissued his book in 1996, he stated in a new preface that were he to write his book again he would give more credit to the role abolitionists played.[4]

To produce valid results in their research, academic historians are trained to seek multiple, independent, written sources before venturing a conclusion about an event. The belief inherent in this practice, that written accounts are of greater validity than oral ones, may need to be modified in certain situations. This is particularly true when the enterprise under investigation was illegal at the time of its occurrence and when a number of its participants were illiterate. Had those who could write about what they were doing done so at the time the activities were taking place, they would have been liable for fines and imprisonment if their writings had been identified. In much the same manner, slaves who could not write had to be careful not to make noise about the fact that they were "fugitives from service." Further, it was in keeping with their ancestral tradition to pass on their experiences in much the manner of the griots who were the keepers and communicators of preliterate African history. Many fugitives living in the Northern states, or a short distance over the border in Canada, were also aware that rewards were offered by former owners for the capture and return of their property and that fraudulent means were used to lure former fugitives into captivity.[5]

It is also reasonable to assess the UGRR based on its similarity to other underground movements, of which it was certainly neither the first nor the last. Throughout the last two millennia, at least, there are ample examples of members of unempowered and oppressed groups being clandestinely aided. Persecuted Christians during the Roman Empire, for example, used the now ubiquitous fish symbol to discreetly and effectively mark gathering places. In more recent times, the Great Depression of the 1930s saw many unemployed men seeking work, "riding the rails" in an effort to find employment. At various freight yards they could find chalked messages indicating which residences in the area were likely to provide food and pocket change to see them along their way. When the traveler reached the street indicated, he would often find another mark indicating the home of a likely donor.

One further indication that a group need not have a corporate table of organization to qualify as organized comes from a *New York Times* article on the role of individual German citizens in saving Jews during the Nazi regime. That article revealed that somewhat more than 5 percent of the 180,000 Jews living in Berlin at that time survived in the city due to efforts on their behalf by non-Jewish residents. With information now emerging about this phenomenon, it is estimated that for every Jew saved, at least seven people must have intervened. Some of the survivors report having more than a score of hiding places, with one survivor, who after the war became the conductor of the Berlin Baroque Orchestra, naming fifty protectors.[6]

While one must be mindful of the roles of great political, economic, and military forces in influencing important events, it should be remembered that individual action can also be an effective force for change. This belief is memorialized in the quotation attributed to Edmund Burke, "For evil to triumph, it is only necessary that good men do nothing."

3

Rumblings in Wisconsin

In 1842, a young, light-skinned slave, Caroline Quarles, escaped from the St. Louis home of her mistress, who was also her aunt. She initiated the escape herself and made it without assistance to a steamboat, where she mingled with a group of schoolgirls, passing as white. Arriving safely at Alton, Illinois, she received immediate assistance from a black man who suggested which stagecoach she should take north. She paid her fare with money she had saved for just such a purpose. Arriving in Milwaukee, she was soon forced to escape the shelter offered by another black man when she learned he was in the employ of her pursuers. She was then moved to Waukesha, Wisconsin, by white abolitionists, who contacted another like-minded person, Dr. Charles Dyer of Burlington, who made up a purse for her from contributions. After being hidden in a number of places in southeastern Wisconsin, she was escorted to Canada by another abolitionist, Lyman Goodnow. They followed a circuitous route through Wisconsin, Illinois, Indiana, and Michigan, finally arriving on the other side of the Detroit River, in Sandwich, Ontario, now Windsor. Goodnow returned to Wisconsin six weeks after he had left with Quarles.

Thirty years later, after Quarles had learned to read and write, she composed letters that included details about her marriage and children. A few years ago, the descendants of Caroline Quarles traveled to Wisconsin from Windsor, where they met the descendants of the Reverend Jonathan Daugherty, one of Caroline's rescuers, to express their gratitude for the help given to their matriarch more than 150 years earlier, assistance that made their lives possible.[1]

Although Wisconsin is not as well known as the eastern states for UGRR activities, there was still considerable action. The first antislavery society in Wisconsin, the Burlington Liberty Association, was founded in 1844 by Dr. E. G. Dyer, who also assisted Caroline Quarles.[2]

Far and away the largest and most vigorous Wisconsin responses to the Fugitive Slave Law occurred in Milwaukee within a few weeks of the passage of the law. There were, of course, the newspaper stories and comments from abolitionist editors such as Sherman Booth of Milwaukee. Beyond that, an event took place that would, for all time, leave no further doubt of the involvement of the primary victims of the Fugitive Slave Law in overturning that law.

On Monday evening, October 7, 1850, the colored citizens of Milwaukee met at a local hall.[3] At this time, about one hundred such persons lived in Milwaukee.[4] That number represented about 1 percent of the population. Lewis Johnson was appointed chairman of the group. Johnson, age thirty-three and a barber, was born in New York and lived in the home of Henry Clarke, a thirty-five-year-old barber who owned the Pioneer Hair Dressing Salon in the heart of downtown. His clientele included a number of the abolitionists who would be involved in Joshua's rescue four years later. He was apparently sufficiently successful in his business that he was able to place a sizable ad in the 1854 city directory.[5]

Johnson opened the meeting by saying:

> The time has arrived when we are all called upon to do our duty to ourselves and our God. By the passage of *a law for the capture of fugitive slaves*, entitled 'An act to amend and supplementary to the act of 1793 respecting fugitives from justice and persons escaping from the service of their masters,' which has become the law of the land, we feel called on to decide for ourselves whether we will tamely submit to this enactment or not. No other alternative is left us but to choose between Liberty or Death. We are also to say whether we will suffer our brethren to be taken back into worse than Egyptian bondage.

Or whether we will swear by High Heaven to rescue them at all hazards, even unto death. These are the questions for you to decide—these are the considerations which have called you together to-night. This is the first meeting of any kind in which the colored people of this State have been called upon to express an opinion. Illinois has spoken and the voice of the great Empire State has reached our ears. Though few in number, let us be faithful to ourselves, to our trembling fugitive brothers, and to our God. Let your resolves be bold, let them come from the heart, speaking the voice of men who are determined upon the resolution of Patrick Henry—"Liberty or Death."[6]

Following the cheers of those assembled, a committee to draft a preamble and resolutions was appointed. The members were Clarke, Alexander Wilson, W. C. Harlan, John Gardner, and William Miner.

While the committee was doing its work, a twenty-two-year-old mason named William Thomas Watson addressed the meeting. Watson lived in the home of his parents, Sully and Susanna Watson, who moved to Milwaukee from Ohio because they had heard they would receive better treatment in Wisconsin than they were getting in Ohio. They were originally from Virginia, where he had been a slave and she, freeborn. Upon earning his freedom, the Watsons were required to leave the state because former slaves could no longer live there, lest it give other slaves the idea that freedom was possible. The freeborn Susanna had learned to read and write and saw to it that her husband and children possessed those skills as well. Among the family's possessions archived in a Milwaukee museum are Sully Watson's freedom papers and an antislavery book published in 1835.[7]

In his address to the meeting's attendees, the young Watson spoke of the dangers of the current conditions, specifically:

our liability to be arrested at almost any moment, and taken we know not where, before we know not whom, and adjudged before any slavish Commissioner or Judge, whose fiat would be omnipotent in deciding us to be chattel property, belonging to any claimant who would commit perjury in swearing to men, women or persons they never saw. In all the bearings of the law, we see no hope, no ray of light except in self protection, which is the law of Heaven.[8]

Joseph H. Barguet, who had been appointed secretary, spoke next. Born in Alabama, probably as a slave, Barguet lived with the family of William Harlan, another member of the committee. He, too, was employed as a mason, one of the many black members of the building trades who helped to construct the city of Milwaukee. One can only imagine the response of the audience as his voice rang through the meeting hall:

> GENTLEMEN: From my heart let me pray you to forget everything like feelings of animosity, forget that you were freeborn, forget, you whose parents wore chains, all differences between you; remember only the hour that has arrived when you, one and all, are called on to do your duty to yourselves and your brothers. Springing from one race, let us make common cause, one with another; let us shield one another; let us die for one another. Let us be ready in all times, in all places, whether in security or danger, to throw our lives in the breach when called on to protect our flying brothers. Remember the slaveholder who seeks to rob him of his all, his life, his liberty, who would rush even unto our hearthstones, and tear from our fond embrace, the children of our loins, yea, the wife of our bosoms. We stand no better chance than the fugitive, and gentlemen, the blood of Nubia is in our cheeks; the fangs of the bloodhound is not particular as to his prey. The law is his; Senator Mason has said it; unworthy of the land that gave him birth. The great charter of human rights, the Habeus [*sic*] Corpus has been broken down. Robbed of every right, every protection, save strong arms and brave hearts, what are we to do? Let us, I say, unite; nature teaches us that the wolves hunt in packs to protect themselves. Gentlemen, before you this night, I pledge my life to come forward at any time, and redeem my word; and once more I would add, be ready, sharpen your swords by the midnight lamp, be in the saddle by the first streak of day. If your liberty is worth having, it is

worth a life to preserve it. But I am intruding on your time; one more word and I am done. How heart-sickening it is to reflect upon our situations. We are Americans by birth; the blush of shame comes to my cheek when I think of it, that the land of our nativity refuses us her protection, while she holds out her wide spread arms to receive a Kossuth, a Paez, Garibaldi and other fugitives, lovers of Liberty and Republicanism. Let us then, as the last resort, point our brethren to the north star. The eagle no longer protects him under the shadow of her wings. Let him go and throw himself under the tender clutches of the British lion. Remember, then, that bayonets may be called upon to uphold such abominations for a time, but surely as the love of freedom swells the hearts of mankind; surely as sweet freedom, once tasted, can never be forgotten, the end of that triumph will be terrible.[9]

As this twenty-seven-year-old freedom fighter concluded his remarks, the resolutions committee returned and their chairman, Henry Clarke, presented to the audience the preamble and seven resolutions that the committee had drafted. In vigorous language, the resolutions condemned the Fugitive Slave Law, vowed to rescue their affected brethren using all means available, thanked Wisconsin's senators and representatives for their opposition to the bill, affirmed pride in Wisconsin for opposing the law, and thanked the newspapers of the state that opposed the law. Speaking of some of the states that had supported the passage of the act, Clarke referred to them as "Old Virginny, Nullifying South Carolina and Disunion Georgia." The assemblage adopted the resolutions unanimously, and the meeting was adjourned.[10]

These few examples from southeastern Wisconsin clearly indicate the presence of several loosely organized groups, both black and white, concerned with the plight of fugitive slaves and willing to involve themselves in various ways on their behalf.

4

Flight to Freedom

TWO HUNDRED DOLLARS REWARD.

RAN away from the subscriber, living 4 miles west of the city of St. Louis, on Saturday night last, a negro man by the name of Joshua; about 35 or 40 years of age, about 6 feet high, spare, with long legs and short body, full suit of hair, eyes inflamed and red; his color is an ashy black. Had on when he went away a pair of black satinet pantaloons, pair of heavy kip boots, an old-fashioned black dress coat, and osnaburg shirt. He took no clothes with him. The above reward will be paid for his apprehension if taken out of the State, and fifty dollars if taken in the State.   B. S. GARLAND.

May 17, 1852.   my18 2w

This reward notice by B. S. Garland for the return of Joshua ran in every issue of the *Missouri Republican* for the last two weeks of May 1852.

It is not known whether a specific event prompted Joshua to escape from his owner when he did. There may have been no single reason, simply the accumulation of the humility of slavery pushing him to the final decision. In any event, he left about May 15, 1852.

Did Joshua, when he made his escape, deliberately head for Racine, Wisconsin, or was he aiming for Canada and remained in Racine because it seemed far enough away to be safe and employment was available? A complete answer to that question will probably never be known—precious little is known about this catalytic event—but it is quite likely that he knew of a place north of Illinois where former slaves lived and that he decided to keep going to put distance between himself and Garland as quickly as he could.

Joshua was certainly aware, as were all slaves, of the consequences of being captured and returned to an owner. Such an event was freely communicated by the owner to the remaining slaves on the farm or plantation, as well as to those in the area, and they were

25

all too painfully aware of the consequences of the failed attempt. Punishments could range all the way from beatings or being placed in collars and shackles to branding, castration, amputation, or being sold south.

The first stage of Joshua's journey was the crossing of the Mississippi River to Alton, Illinois. There were two churches in St. Louis actively engaged in aiding fugitive slaves. One of these was German, the other, colored. Moored in the Mississippi River between St. Louis and Alton was a barge that was used as a school for black children. This barge also served as a hiding place for slaves, and at night it could be moved some distance to transport fugitives to the Illinois shore.[1]

When Joshua left the service of Benammi Garland in the spring of 1852, he had undoubtedly thought about it for some time. Whether or not the reason he later gave for leaving was the actual one, it did provide a reasonable presumption that his owner was not in residence when he left. While in custody during his brief captivity in 1854, Joshua told Deputy U.S. Marshal Charles C. Cotton that he had been drinking for a week and, when he sobered up, he was afraid to return to the farm.[2] Because this statement was made after his capture and as an explanation to his owner, in part to relieve the severity of his anticipated punishment, its truthfulness may be in doubt. Moreover, because the first fugitive slave notice appeared in the *Missouri Republican* on Wednesday, May 19, 1852, and stated that Joshua had left on the previous Saturday, it is somewhat unlikely that Garland was in town at the time, or he would have arranged for an earlier notice. He also ran the notice every day until the end of the month.

However he accomplished it, Joshua did make it across the river and followed what was known as the "Drinkin' Gourd." Slaves learned routes to freedom navigating by the North Star, which they located by using the stars of the Big Dipper; slaves knew the Dipper as the "Drinkin' Gourd," because a hollowed-out gourd is what they used to dip and drink water. It was not an easy journey. He probably left with only the clothes on his back.

Runaway slaves, traveling by themselves, typically traveled by night and tried to find some concealment for sleep in the daytime. Joshua later reported that after he had crossed the river at Alton, a woman on a farm provided him with some seed potatoes for food on his journey. He also said that at one point, he went three days without food.[3] No documentation is available stating how long it took him to arrive in Racine or where he may have stopped along the way. Fugitive slaves, on average, traveled eight to ten miles a day, unless they were fortunate enough to get a wagon ride with someone sympathetic to their plight. With the distance between St. Louis and Racine being somewhat more than 350 miles, one can estimate a probable journey of at least six to seven weeks, unless there were extended stopovers.

The route Joshua took could easily have been a northeast one through Jacksonville, Farmington, Princeton, Paw Paw, Aurora, and St. Charles, Illinois, leading him to Lake County, which borders Wisconsin. He could also have followed the course of the Rock, Fox, or Des Plaines Rivers, leading him to Beloit, Rochester, or Union Grove, Wisconsin. All of these towns had associations with abolitionists and the UGRR. These routes would have bypassed Chicago, which was known to be heavily patrolled and posted with notices offering rewards for the return of a fugitive, as had been the case with Caroline Quarles when she was attempting to reach Canada. Such a reward, sometimes as high as three hundred dollars, might be the equivalent of a year's wages for a free working man.

Whatever route he traveled, Joshua is likely to have arrived in Racine in the late spring or early summer of 1852, beginning what he hoped would be a life of freedom from both slavery and fear of capture.

One of the first, and most significant, things he did upon arrival was to select a surname for himself. In general, a slave was not permitted to have a family name. To allow such a custom would have diluted the concept of the slave as chattel and would have raised his status above that of the owner's horses and family pets. The closest he would have come to having a second name would occur when another owner might refer to him as "Mr. Garland's boy, Joshua."

In selecting a surname, he would not choose Garland, because of the greater risk of discovery by slave hunters. The name he did select, however, may not have been the safest choice either. He called himself "Joshua Glover."

Evidence exists that this may not have been a random choice. Garland's slaves share a page of the 1850 Census Slave Schedule with the slaves of Martha Glover, a widow, originally from South Carolina. That she also lived near Garland's farm is evidenced by her presence within a couple of pages of Garland's in the regular enumeration for that year. She owned a dozen and a half slaves, twelve of whom were under the age of eighteen.[4] Unlike Garland, she was not listed in the most recent agricultural schedule and may therefore be presumed not to have been engaged in farming. Because she was not earning income from agriculture, one must consider whether she was renting slaves to others, raising them for sale, or closing down the farm and disposing of her assets. She does not appear in the 1860 census for that area of St. Louis.

Later in this story, a federal marshal would testify that Joshua Glover had told him that his owner previous to Garland had been "a widow lady. However," the marshal continued, "I disremember her name."[5] The fact that the auction at which Joshua was purchased was a probate auction—that is, one in which bequeathed property was sold—is a further indication that the widowed Martha Glover was probably Joshua's previous owner.

5

Life in Racine

Gilbert Knapp left his home on Cape Cod, in the town of Chatham, Massachusetts, when he was fifteen years old. The year was 1813, and he set to sea on a ship known as a privateer during the War of 1812. During his tour he heard much about the Great Lakes and the advantages of a career on a revenue cutter, an armed government vessel often used to enforce revenue laws. In 1819, Knapp secured a job as captain of a revenue cutter. On one of his postwar trips on Lake Michigan, he came upon the mouth of the Root River, then known as the Chippecotton. Impressed with the fertile, virgin territory, he promised himself he would return. It took him another nine years to get back there, and when he did, in 1828, he was still impressed with the possibilities for both settlement and a harbor. In 1834, he was finally able to purchase land and establish a trading post.[1]

The following year Knapp moved to the trading post with his family, a journey that could take many weeks, whether traveling by land or water. Strange as it may appear to those who now consider the West to begin somewhere around Colorado, Racine in the early nineteenth century was the Far West and was initially populated by easterners, many of them having come from strongly abolitionist New England and upstate New York. These were the sort of men for whom the term "rugged individualists" was coined. Obstacles were considered by them as things to be removed from their paths by whatever means were available, even if those means would not be entirely legal outside the loosely controlled territories.

One of Knapp's first acts was to construct two shanties and call them a courthouse and a jail so a settlement could be legally organized. Within three years, a thriving community of some three hundred people was living and working in the hamlet he had named Port Gilbert. When Knapp laid claim to the land he had settled, he had in his possession a total of 141 acres. He changed the name of the river from Chippecotton to Root, because the name described the many tree roots in the river. The town was then named Racine, the French word for root.[2]

On and off throughout his stay in Racine, Knapp was commissioned the captain of a revenue cutter, depending on whether the Whigs were in or out of office. Knapp brought this seesaw career on himself. In 1828, when he was working on a cutter out of Erie, Pennsylvania, and Andrew Jackson was running for the presidency, Knapp told a group of people, "I consider General Jackson a cutthroat and a murderer, and his wife a strumpet, and if he should be elected I will never hold an appointment under him."[3]

Knapp's words were prophetic. When Jackson was elected, Knapp lost his commission. He was in again with William Henry Harrison, out with James Polk, and in with Zachary Taylor. His business ventures also had their ups and downs. In early 1838 he was one of the incorporators of the county's first state-chartered railway system. The project fell through and was never completed. The county's first newspaper, in which he was an investor, lasted less than one year. He had better luck when he and a group of town fathers incorporated the Racine and Rock River Plank Road, which ran from the heart of Racine to Janesville, some fifty miles distant.[4]

This road opened the surrounding territory to farmers who could transport their produce to Racine for shipment to Milwaukee, Chicago, and the East. The initial subscription for this road was seventy-four thousand dollars. The amount of tolls received from its opening in June 1849 until the end of November was a bit less than forty-five hundred dollars. At a toll of one cent per mile, the directors were able to declare to the subscribers a dividend of one cent a mile per month through November.[5]

Such roads developed an additional use, one that was not originally intended. Fugitive slaves traveling to Racine from Illinois could make better time on these roads on their way north than if they had to struggle through the heavy oak forests and rutted paths that covered the area. Alfred Payne, a local resident, was a toll collector on the portion of the road that ran from Racine to Burlington and would later play a role in the journey of Joshua Glover on the UGRR.[6]

By 1847 the three hundred residents had increased almost tenfold to twenty-nine hundred.[7] By the time Glover arrived in town in 1852, Racine was a thriving community of more than five thousand people.[8] The combination of trading post, plank road, and harbor had gradually convinced people to live in Racine. There were four newspapers, including one in German. Charles Clement, who became the editor of the abolitionist paper the *Racine Advocate* in 1853, would play a significant role in Glover's life. Of the almost dozen and a half churches, two served the colored population. While the Reverend Zebulon Humphrey, pastor of First Presbyterian Church and a noted abolitionist, who was believed to harbor fugitive slaves in the church basement, might have welcomed Glover to the congregation, it is more likely that Glover attended the Colored Baptist Church, led by the Reverend Pleasant Bowler and located on Campbell between Eleventh and Twelfth Streets.[9] Racine might well have been a hotbed of abolitionist sympathizers, but most of the white populace still preferred to celebrate the Sabbath with those of their own color.

During the daytime, the heart of activity in the city was located around Haymarket Square, now known as Monument Square. It was there and at the harbor, a short distance northeast, that the commercial life of the city hummed along. Racine at that time was not a community that any contemporary resident would recognize. There were no paved streets, although there were some boardwalks. On a rainy spring day, a woman who ventured into town would be guaranteed muddy skirts, which would have to be laundered later by her, her live-in servant, if she could afford one, or one of the colored women who took in washing.

Justinian Cartwright, one of the prominent colored citizens of Racine, was married to a white woman and had five children. It is likely that his mother-in-law also lived with the family.[10] He was a blacksmith, as were two of his sons later, and he ran a thriving business in the town. He also came from a background of slavery in

Haymarket Square was the site of the protest meeting held in Racine on the day following Glover's capture.

Kentucky and had been at the battle of New Orleans as a waiting boy for General Andrew Jackson.[11] His familiarity with the rigors of slavery, as well as his position as a respected member of the colored community, would have made him a likely source of employment information for Glover when he arrived in town. Glover would also often come into town on Saturdays to sell articles he had made and would undoubtedly stop for conversation and gossip at Cartwright's shop, a sure source of information and news for blacks.[12] Such a practice would not be unfamiliar to Glover, as it was the custom of a number of Southern slave owners to give their slaves Saturday afternoon off to sell their handmade crafts. Some of this money might have to be remitted to the owner, while a portion could be kept by the slave for his own purposes.[13] The money saved in this way was sometimes used by the slave to purchase his or her freedom.

When night fell, most normal activity in the town ceased. There were no streetlights. In fact, although a contract had been given to provide gas lamps in 1853, the contractor could not get started right away, and lights did not appear on the streets of Racine until 1857. Filled with enthusiasm over the rapid growth of their town, the council passed a resolution to purchase seventy lamps at a cost of more than twenty-five hundred dollars. The public, appalled at the cost, protested, and the council finally settled on thirty lamps for less than one thousand dollars. A light tender was appointed to turn off all the lamps at midnight, and on moonlit nights they were not turned on at all.[14]

Besides the light of the moon, when it was available, there was sometimes another, less welcome source of illumination. That was the unnatural light of the numerous fires that plagued Racine as well as many of the towns in the West, whose structures were built primarily of wood. The frequency of such events led to the formation of many volunteer fire companies, which often vied with each other to be the first to arrive at a fire. When someone noticed that a fire had broken out, a triangle was beaten and the bells were rung at the courthouse and at the Baptist church to call out the fire companies. Of the members, one or two were appointed to prepare a hot meal for the company following its return from the fire. These postfire celebrations often got out of hand when the firefighters, flushed with success after their work, also became flushed with alcohol. These companies also evolved into clubs whose balls became the social events of the season. At times the city government disbanded one company or another as a result of its raucous behavior, as occurred when a hook and ladder company, which had been disbanded several times, was once again disciplined when one of its members was killed at a postfire carousal.[15]

When Glover arrived in Racine, after his nearly four hundred-mile journey from Garland's farm, he may not have appraised it with the same businesslike and aesthetic eye as Gilbert Knapp had done, but he was undoubtedly grateful to have found a resting place at last. He knew that he could never completely relax as long as the Fugitive Slave Law commanded all to assist his owner in his return. Nonetheless, almost four hundred miles was a considerable and, he probably imagined, safe distance to allow him to consider settling down and getting a job.

As with many fugitive slaves who headed for Canada, Glover did not arrive in Racine ignorant of its reputation as an antislavery town. The town's colored residents likely greeted Glover with additional insights, such as which white people could be trusted and of whom he should be wary. He was probably told that

Duncan Sinclair owned a lumberyard in town and was known to hire fugitive slaves at his mill.

To get to the Rice and Sinclair mill, which was located on the rapids of the Root River about four miles from town, Glover needed to head north. As he made his way from the main part of town, located south of the river, he likely observed much about the geography of Racine and who lived where. It would not take him long to discover that the larger and more magnificent homes were located on the south side and close to the lake. It was here that the movers and shakers lived: Charles Clement, the newspaper editor; A. P. Dutton, the grain merchant and freight forwarder; Mark Miller, bookshop owner and publisher of Racine's first city directory; and Duncan Sinclair, who would soon become Glover's employer.[16]

Glover's first problem would have arisen when he had to cross the river to get to the north side of town. There had once been a small bridge there, but it had been washed away in 1843. Walking a block west of the main street to Wisconsin Street revealed a scow moored between two piers; the large, flat-bottomed boat served as a bridge, which was moved out of the channel whenever a ship needed to pass. It would not be until 1853 that a permanent structure was built at that spot, barely wide enough for a team to pass and having no walk for foot passengers and no rail to protect a pedestrian from falling in on a windy day.[17]

Having safely crossed the river, Glover would have then been introduced to the north side, a place of cheap lots and tiny houses. Living there were the poor, recent immigrants, and other "persons of no importance," as they were referred to in a history of the area. They lived on the corn and beans that grew in their front yards and on the geese and swine that roamed the grassy streets between their fences. These people were the town's laborers, tree cutters, house builders, wheat handlers, and dray men, hauling the city's goods on one-horse wagons. Important as they were to the city's economy, they were not important enough to require that a decent bridge be built so they could travel safely from home to work and back.[18]

Arriving finally at the mill on the banks of the Root River, Glover was probably offered somewhere between fifty cents and a dollar a day as a laborer, an average amount. In exchange for this wage he turned trees into boards to supply Sinclair's lumber business with the materials required to meet Racine's growing need for ships and houses.

The owners of the sawmill provided Glover with living quarters, a small shanty near the river, with the rent probably deducted from his pay. His home had one feature that had not been present in any other place he had lived: a bolt on the inside of his door, assuring him privacy, a privilege available only to a free man. While his wages would never make him a rich man, it was the first time he had ever been paid for his labor in his own name. He could quit his job and find another one if he chose. He could fish in the Root River, both for his food and for the pleasure of it. He could, at times, stop work briefly to enjoy the sight of the trees against the sky and not worry that he would be threatened with punishment for being a "lazy nigger." Even though he might still work from "can't see to can't see," he did so as a free man. When he had leisure time, he could use it as he wished, which might include spending time with a woman.

The joys of freedom notwithstanding, Glover could not forget that he was a fugitive slave with a price on his head. It would also be apparent to any passerby that he was not as well clothed as Cartwright the blacksmith, or Rubin Rollins the grocer, or Samuel Jackson the barber, or many of the other colored tradesmen living in Racine.[19]

Should he for a brief time forget, there would be many occasions for Glover to be reminded when there were rumors of slave catchers in town. There were other less threatening but nonetheless pressing reminders of his status. Although it's not likely that he would have been called "nigger" to his face, he would have overheard even the abolitionists, in their conversations with each other, use the term "darky."

Prominent among Glover's concerns would have been the thought of capture and return—not just to St. Louis but possibly to the fate of being sold down the river, where slaves were treated even more harshly. While Thomas Jefferson did not have Joshua Glover, or his ilk, in mind when he said, "Eternal vigilance is the price of liberty," Glover would have had no difficulty agreeing with the sentiment.

For about two years, Glover lived and worked in Racine, gradually relaxing as he came to know the town and its people, as well as the friends of his own race that he had made. What he did not know was that one of the men he considered a friend would be his undoing, brought on, in part perhaps, by his own behavior.

6

A Violent Capture and Thrilling Escape

Approximately sixty black and mulatto adult citizens were recorded as living in Racine in the 1850 U.S. census. Of these, about two dozen were listed as having been born in states permitting slavery.[1] Because they were all too aware of the precarious nature of the conditions under which they lived, those who were runaway slaves would have been especially wary about disclosing their actual state of origin or might have avoided the enumerator as he made his rounds, as is done to this day by those called "undocumented aliens." Though they lived in a free state, hundreds of miles from the site of their bondage, Racine's black residents knew they could very quickly be returned to involuntary servitude. For Joshua Glover, this danger hit particularly close to home. On or about March 8, 1854, two men were seen attempting to enter Glover's cabin; finding it locked, they left. A colored woman who had seen them, thinking she might be the target of their efforts, left town that night.[2]

Such fear was not unfounded. It was relatively easy for an owner to "reclaim" a runaway slave just as soon as the owner could satisfy a federal judge that the person in question was someone other than who he or she claimed to be.

That is exactly what Benammi Garland did shortly after arriving in Milwaukee from St. Louis in early March. Accompanied by Police Officer Melvin, also of St. Louis, Garland visited the law offices of Arnold and Hamilton, retaining the services of Jonathan

37

E. Arnold. This was probably the same Jonathan Arnold who was retained in 1842 by the former owners of Caroline Quarles, who hid in Milwaukee before she was taken to Canada on the UGRR. The same issue of the paper that reported that meeting also reported that Arnold's associate, Mr. Hamilton, approached Captain Gardiner of the militia in an effort to borrow twelve revolvers, to be used for protection against the angry abolitionists that were anticipated. He was adamantly refused.[3]

At the attorneys' office, Garland executed an affidavit attesting to his ownership of Glover. Prior to his arrival in Milwaukee, Garland had made proof of his property before the Court of Common Pleas in St. Louis, during its February term.[4] This was then presented to Andrew G. Miller, the federal judge for the Milwaukee district, who issued a warrant for the arrest of Glover. Document in hand, Garland proceeded to Racine in the company of Officer Melvin and Deputy U.S. Marshal Charles C. Cotton. Once there, Garland added others to the group so the posse would be of sufficient size and strength to assure Glover's capture. They were joined by Deputy Marshal Kearney and by a fifth person, Daniel F. Houghton, a farmer from the nearby town of Dover.

No available accounts indicate that Houghton, a Democrat, also known to the community as "the Slave Catcher of Dover," took any more active role in the capture than being on the scene. He was also said to have aspirations to be the next state senator from the county.[5] He and his wife, Emily, both thirty, as well as the two eldest of their three children, were born in New York. Their youngest, a year old, was born in Wisconsin, indicating that the family had lived there only a few years. Houghton also had living in his household two other people, Charles and Jane Robinson, ages sixty-two and forty-eight, respectively, both born in New York and both black. If their ages were listed correctly, they would have been born in 1788 and 1802 and might well have also been born into slavery in New York. Although under state law Jane Robinson would have been considered free, she would still have been required to serve her mother's owner until she reached the age of twenty-five.[6]

In one newspaper account following Glover's capture, Houghton was referred to as "an old Hunker Democrat from the town of Dover."[7] Another incident is related sometime after the capture of Glover in which Houghton stopped at a tavern in the county and offered to buy a drink for the man standing next to him at the bar. After the offer was refused by him, and successively by every man at the bar, the last one to refuse declared loudly, "No one here will drink with a nigger catcher."[8] It is also an interesting sidelight that when Houghton was arrested on state charges of kidnapping following Glover's capture, his bail was put up by A. P. Dutton, the Racine grain merchant and transfer agent who later figured prominently in Glover's journey to Canada.[9]

As the sun was beginning to set, Garland and the posse arranged to hire two wagons at the Armour Livery Stable, located in Racine. Climbing into the wagons as dusk gathered, the party headed for Glover's quarters at the Rice and Sinclair sawmill, about four miles from town.[10] The late winter weather had been marked by alternating freezing and thawing, and there had been a recent heavy snowfall as well, producing conditions not very conducive to either stealth or speed, both of which were essential for the success of their mission. In fact, the weather in the area was so miserable, and the streets in such desperate condition, that a local newspaper reported that attendance at Friday's opening of *Uncle Tom's Cabin* in Milwaukee was considerably lower than expected, although the next issue noted that Saturday's performance was well attended and the audience seemed highly gratified.[11]

The posse had, however, an ace in the hole because of the presence in Glover's cabin of Nelson Turner. A freed slave from Natchez, Mississippi, Turner is believed to have made a couple of trips to St. Louis over the previous winter to consult with Garland and had accompanied Garland and Melvin from St. Louis to Racine on their mission to capture Glover. After his arrival, he had also been observed to meet with Marshal Kearney.[12]

Turner showed up at Glover's cabin with a bottle of whiskey—which had been supplied by Garland—a deck of cards, and another colored man, William Alby. The fact that slave catchers were known to be in town would almost certainly have put Glover on the alert. In addition, there were rumors circulating that Glover was romancing Turner's wife. If that was true, Glover would perhaps have been even more suspicious of Turner's generosity. He bolted the door of

his cabin before sitting down to play cards. He also drank very spar-
ingly that evening.

Arriving in the area of the mill, the party left their wagons
about a hundred yards from the small shanty occupied by Glover
and his companions. As the men stealthily approached the cabin,
the crunching sounds of their footsteps in the hard snow somewhat
muffled by the nearby rapids of the Root River, Garland readied his
pistol. Cotton took out his manacles, leaving his pistol in his
pocket, and Kearney tightened his grip on the whip he carried. One
of the men knocked loudly on the door. As Turner rose to go to
the door, Glover was heard to call out, "Don't open it 'til we know
who's there!"[13]

Ignoring the warning, Turner drew the bolt and flung open the
door, permitting Garland, Cotton, and Kearney to rush in. Glover
sprang to his feet and, seizing Garland's hand, attempted to wrest
the pistol from him. Seeing the struggle between master and slave,
Marshal Cotton dealt Glover a sharp blow to the head with his
handcuffs, causing a severe scalp wound. Marshal Kearney, in the
meantime, struck Glover with the butt end of the whip. The force
of this combined onslaught drove Glover to the floor, where he lay
dazed and bleeding profusely. While Glover was being subdued,
Alby apparently slipped away, leaving Turner as the only other
occupant of the cabin to observe the melee.[14]

As Glover, his hands manacled, was led by his captors to one of
the wagons, he appeared to recognize Garland for the first time.
Marshal Cotton, in later court testimony, said Glover expressed his
willingness to return with Garland to St. Louis. When asked by
Garland why he had left, Glover said that he had been on a drinking spree, and that he was away from home from Friday to the next
Saturday. When he sobered up he left the neighborhood and
crossed the Mississippi because he became afraid that he would be
sold down the river.[15]

That slaves learned to say the things they knew their owners
wanted to hear, especially when it might mitigate their anticipated
punishment, is further demonstrated by a similar event that took
place in the life of Anthony Burns. A fugitive slave from Virginia,
Burns was captured in May 1854 by his owner, Charles Suttle, in
Boston. Asked why he had run away, Burns told a story about acci-

dentally falling asleep while working on a ship in the harbor and awakening when it arrived in Boston. Following that rationalization, he expressed his willingness to return with his master.[16] To convince everyone of his willingness to comply, he had to play along with a not-uncommon scenario. When Suttle visited Burns in his cell, he asked a number of questions such as, "Did I ever whip you, Anthony?" and "Did I not, when you were sick, take my bed from my own house for you?" The expected answers from Burns would demonstrate Suttle to be a kindly master who was always concerned with his bondsman's welfare.[17] This fictive interplay between master and slave thus sometimes served the double purpose of easing the slave's punishment while reassuring the owner that he himself was a fine fellow.

It also explains why Glover expressed immediate interest in returning to St. Louis with Garland. If Glover had disclosed any deliberate intent to deprive Garland of his services, he would almost certainly have received more severe punishment upon his return to St. Louis. Many owners also needed to believe that their slaves were treated fairly, the very obvious contradiction presented by slavery's mere existence notwithstanding.

But however willing Glover might have initially been to return with Garland, there is one way in which he certainly defied the man who claimed to own him. Whether this was conscious defiance remains unknown. On a note appended to the warrant signed by Marshal S. R. Abelman, Deputy Marshall Cotton wrote, "I have apprehended the within named Joshua Glover and have him in custody, March 11, 1854." An additional note dated two o'clock in the afternoon on Saturday, March 11, 1854, and signed by Judge Andrew Miller states: "Ordered that the case of Benammi Garland against Joshua Glover is set down for hearing on Monday morning at ten o'clock."[18] These two comments appear to be the first written evidence of Joshua having acquired a surname, an act of defiance in the eyes of the scene's St. Louisans. It also indicates that Garland, who had asked that the warrant be issued, had to, for the moment at least, accept the fact that his former slave had two names. Had Garland been successful in his efforts to get Glover back, Joshua would have returned to Missouri leaving his surname in Racine.

Back at the site of Glover's capture outside the cabin, the escaped slave, hatless and in shirtsleeves, was put on the floor of the open wagon and covered by a buffalo robe, his head between Garland's knees. Blood ran down the side of his face, staining his striped shirt.[19] As the occupants of the wagons prepared to leave, his captors decided not to lodge Glover in Racine's small jail that night. It was felt that its size, as well as the multitude of abolitionist sympathizers in town, made it much more vulnerable to an assault in an effort to secure Glover's release. They would instead attempt the approximately twenty-five-mile drive to Milwaukee. One wagon was then returned to the livery stable, while the other, with Turner also in it, headed north. After it had traveled a short distance, Turner was let out, and he disappeared into the night.[20]

Turner's fate following his disappearance from the wagon is unknown, as is the amount of compensation he received from Garland for his efforts, which could have been as much as the two hundred dollars originally offered by Garland when he published his notice regarding Glover's escape. One report states that Turner was later hung by a group of abolitionists.[21] Another account related that a group, unhappy with his role in the capture of Glover, had in turn captured Turner and sold him south.[22] Whatever his fate, it is clear from contemporary accounts that he would have been in considerable danger had he remained in town.

After letting Turner out, the wagon continued on its course to Milwaukee, which had a larger and stronger jail. But the journey did not go as planned. Due to the snow and ice, darkness, and the need to avoid well-traveled routes, the party took a wrong turn and spent the rest of the night trying to find their way north to Milwaukee. They eventually arrived in town about three o'clock in the morning, several hours past their expected arrival time. If the Drinkin' Gourd, which had guided Glover north, had not been obscured by the overcast sky, perhaps they would have arrived sooner. This might have allowed Garland to complete his business more quickly and return with Glover to St. Louis with the speed and secrecy he had hoped for. This delay was only one factor in a series of unanticipated events that would very quickly change the course of Glover's story.

Around the same time the slave catchers were wandering around the countryside trying to find their way to Milwaukee, news of Glover's capture began to circulate through Racine. At approximately ten o'clock in the evening, Charles Rice, one of Glover's employers at the mill, rode into town and reported to Charles Clement, the editor of the abolitionist newspaper the *Racine Advocate*, that Glover had been "kidnapped" from his cabin and was being taken to Milwaukee. Clement quickly arranged for a brief article to appear in his paper on Saturday morning announcing news of the capture. Immediately below that bulletin, it was also reported that the Reverend Zebulon Humphrey, pastor of First Presbyterian Church, would give a discourse on "the moral and religious bearings of the Nebraska Question" at Sunday services.[23] The topic was directed at the proposed Kansas-Nebraska Act, which would allow the voting citizens of newly admitted states to elect whether their state would allow slavery within its borders. Such a sermon, from a clergyman noted for his abolitionist sympathies to a congregation that required prospective members to swear they had not owned slaves, serves to emphasize how seriously many in Racine regarded slavery. It also indicates how the article, paired with news of Glover's capture, so strongly affected those with abolitionist sympathies in Racine.

Clement did not limit the news to Racine. He also telegraphed Sherman Booth, editor of the abolitionist newspaper the *Milwaukee Free Democrat*, to inform him of the "kidnapping," so that he could alert other abolitionists to the events about to take place in their city. Booth would play a pivotal role in the story, perhaps the most crucial one of all, for he would light the kindling that would fuel the next day's events.

Sherman Booth was born in 1812 in Davenport, New York, about forty miles southwest of the capitol at Albany. That part of the state produced many abolitionists who joined the move westward in the 1830s and 1840s. In 1848 he moved to Waukesha, Wisconsin, where he worked for the abolitionist newspaper the *American Freeman*. He purchased it, changed its name to the *Wisconsin Freeman*, and moved it to Milwaukee, renaming it the *Free Democrat*. During these years, he was also an organizer of the Free

Democrat Party, which arose in opposition to the proslavery Democratic Party and was a forerunner of the Republican Party. While living in New York, he was also a temperance leader and active in the Liberty Party, another predecessor of the Republican Party. As a student at Yale, he was one of those selected to teach English to the slaves from the *Amistad*, who were in jail awaiting trial following their attempt to avoid being sent as slaves to Cuba.[24] Booth's ardent interest in Glover's fate would help to sway public opinion in the slave's favor.

By nine o'clock Saturday morning, Booth had word of what had happened in Racine and set about alerting the citizens of Milwaukee. First, however, he needed to find out what had actually happened. He went to the clerk of the federal district court, who directed him to Judge Andrew G. Miller. On the way he met Deputy Marshal Cotton and asked him if he had arrested a colored man the previous night in Racine. Cotton, with what Booth later described as "such perfect *sang froid* [*sic*]," denied any knowledge of such an event, leading Booth to think his Racine informant might be mistaken. On arriving at the judge's office, however, he learned that a warrant had been issued two days earlier for a fugitive slave. Like Cotton, Judge Miller was also reluctant to impart any information to Booth regarding an arrest. After denying any knowledge of whether an arrest had taken place and whether, if it had, the fugitive would appear before him or a U.S. court commissioner, he did agree to permit Booth to be present if adjudication took place.[25]

As the judge presiding over Glover's case, Andrew G. Miller had ultimate judicial control over the fate of Glover. Born in Carlisle, Pennsylvania, in 1801 on land purchased from William Penn, Miller was raised in the same area above the panhandle of Maryland from which the family of Isabelle Cresap Garland, Benammi Garland's wife, had come.

On the way back to his office, Booth ran into General Hortensius Paine, the father of Byron Paine, an attorney who would later represent Booth. Paine told him that Glover was in the county jail. On behalf of Glover, Gen. Paine made application for a writ of habeas corpus and gave it to Marshal O'Brien to be served on Sheriff Page and Marshal Cotton. Booth then went back to his office and had the following handbill made up to distribute throughout the city.

MAN CAPTURED
OUR JAIL USED FOR THE SLAVE-CATCHERS!
Last night a colored man was arrested near
Racine, on a warrant of Judge Miller by
Deputy Sheriff Cotton and making some
resistance, was knocked down and brought
to this City, and incarcerated in the County
Jail. Marshal Cotton denied knowing anything
about it at 9 o'clock this morning. The object
evidently is to get him a secret trial without
giving him a chance to defend himself by counsel.
Citizens of Milwaukee! Shall we have Star
Chamber proceedings here? And shall a man
be dragged back to Slavery from our Free Soil,
without an open trial of his right to Liberty?
Watch your jail, your District and U. S.
Comissioners' Courts!
Milwaukee, March 11, 1854[26]

Back in Racine, the news of Glover's arrest spread rapidly, including the news that he was now being held in a Milwaukee jail. The information incited immediate action. With the bell to the courthouse ringing, the largest group ever to assemble in the city's history gathered in Haymarket Square. From there, events unfolded with rapidity. Committees were appointed and resolutions were adopted demanding a fair and impartial jury trial for Glover and resolving to secure his unconditional release by all honorable means. A warrant was issued for the arrest of Garland and Cotton for assault and battery on Glover, and a committee of one hundred delegates was appointed to accompany the sheriff to Milwaukee to bring them back to face charges.[27] Such an action, an outright defiance of federal law, could result in imprisonment if convicted. That as many as one hundred adult males were willing to undergo this risk gives some idea of the strength of abolitionist sentiment in this frontier town of five thousand.

Shortly before quarter of two in the afternoon, just as the abolitionist contingent from Racine was making plans to embark by steamboat for Milwaukee, Sherman Booth made the news public in Milwaukee. Mounting his horse, he rode up Spring, West Water, and Third Streets to the foot of the hill; crossed the river; and rode down East Water Street to the Fifth Ward and back through Main and Milwaukee Streets, calling out, "Free citizens who do not wish to be made slaves or slave-catchers meet at Courthouse Square at two o'clock!" By the time Booth arrived at the square, people were gathering by the thousands. By two thirty, between three thousand and five thousand people were in attendance, with the lower end of the estimate being supplied primarily by those opposed to any action to free Glover. A vigilance committee of twenty-five was appointed to see that Glover's rights were protected. They numbered among them many of the leading citizens of the city, including the son of General Paine, Byron Paine, who later became counsel for Sherman Booth and then, still later, a justice of the Wisconsin Supreme Court. John Rycraft, a lawyer who, along with Booth, would be indicted by the federal government for aiding and abetting the rescue of Glover, was also present.[28]

A subcommittee, waiting to learn how Judge Miller would proceed in the case, was told about three o'clock that Glover would remain in jail until Monday morning at ten o'clock. At that time he would be brought before Miller for a fair hearing, the judge having previously denied the authority of the state courts to take a prisoner out of the hands of the United States officers. Because the abolitionists believed it was inhumane to keep Glover in jail over the Sabbath and that, under cover of darkness, he might be spirited out of jail by marshals, efforts were made to secure an earlier hearing. These efforts proved unsuccessful, and as the crowd continued to grow, so did the sense of outrage. The militia and fire companies were called to prevent a riot, but only one company of forty men obeyed the summons. Unable to control the crowd, they were dismissed by their officer.[29]

As the afternoon progressed, the speech making and responses from the crowd became so loud that it began to interfere with the business of the circuit court, and the speakers, feeling a need to comply with the law, moved to the roof of the clerk's office so they

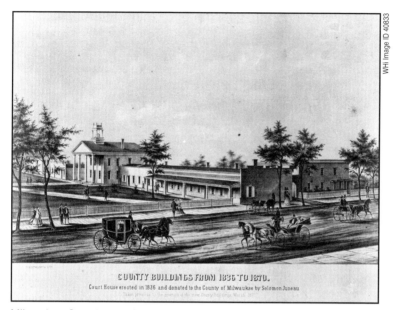

WHi Image ID 40833

COUNTY BUILDINGS FROM 1836 TO 1870.
Court House erected in 1836 and donated to the County of Milwaukee by Solomon Juneau

Milwaukee Courthouse Square, 1854. The jail from which Glover was rescued is in the long building to the right of the Courthouse.

would be less of a disturbance. Many speakers were heard, including A. L. Bielfeld, speaking in German for the benefit of those in that large ethnic group who did not speak English.[30] A portion of the German population of Milwaukee was noted for its strong free-soil views. They were concerned with keeping slavery out of the western territories primarily for economic reasons rather than for philosophical ones.

It was fast approaching five o'clock when the group of abolitionists from Racine disembarked from the steamship and walked in procession to the courthouse. As they arrived, Charles K. Watkins, another attorney with abolitionist leanings, was speaking to the assemblage, insisting there were times when the people must take the law into their own hands or themselves become slaves. Whether the present was such a time, he exhorted, was for them to judge. This was followed by further fiery rhetoric from Booth, who also took care, publicly and loudly, to advise his listeners not to violate the law, as he had consistently done each time he spoke that afternoon.[31] This was clearly one more attempt on his part to distance himself from a possible future charge of inciting the crowd to riot.

The inflammatory rhetoric of the speakers, coupled with the news that Glover would not receive an early hearing, moved the crowd closer to a flash point. Booth, perhaps trying to forestall a precipitous act by the crowd, announced that the Racine delegation and the Vigilance Committee would meet at the American House Hotel to consult as to the proper course to be pursued.

But before that sizable body could even begin to move in the direction of the hotel, the crowd began to rush toward the jail. One man kicked in the outer door. Others used pickaxes to knock down the wall by the side of the guard door.[32] While this melee was occurring, others demanded the keys to the jail. James Angove, about thirty-one years old and a mason, heard the demands for keys and turned in the direction of nearby St. John's Cathedral, then in the process of construction.[33] Noticing a pile of lumber, he picked up a beam about six inches around and said to the crowd, "Here's a good enough key."[34] Several other men, including one George Bingham, seized the makeshift battering ram and breached the stronghold.[35] Within the ground-floor jail, Glover could probably hear the tumult and imagine that rescue was imminent. A few moments later, the men burst through. Just as suddenly as he had been captured the night before, Glover was released from his bonds. He waved his hat at the crowd as he was delivered from his cell by members of the rescue party.[36]

Glover's exultation wasn't the only thing that impressed those watching. As Angove saw Glover being removed from the jail, he was so struck by Glover's apparent strength that he wondered how his captors had been able to arrest him in the first place.[37] Sheriff Conover said later that he tried to detain Glover at the break-in, but some men pulled him away after a scuffle.[38]

Back in Racine people were still waiting on the square for further news from Milwaukee. Several telegraphic dispatches were received late Saturday evening, announcing news of the incredible rescue of Glover from jail. As the *Racine Advocate* reported the next morning, when the waiting crowd received the news, "[O]ne universal expression of satisfaction burst forth . . . and cannon were fired, bonfires lighted, bands of music patrolled the streets and every demonstration was made . . . at the triumph of humanity over brutality and the slave driver's power."[39]

From the moment that Glover appeared in public in front of the Milwaukee jail, his progress through the city was part flight and part triumphal parade. His blood-encrusted head was the first view the crowd had of him as his rescuers carried him to the waiting express wagon, which was drawn by two horses. People crowded around the wagon, trying to shake Glover's hand, amid many cheers from those assembled. About fifteen hours earlier he had arrived in Milwaukee in shackles, under cover of darkness, terrified of being returned to his master. Now he was being treated as a conquering hero. Onlookers suggested getting warmer clothing for him, but in the interest of a speedy getaway it was decided to forgo the kindness.

Witnesses reported various occupants in the wagon, in addition to Glover, as it made its way south and west from the jail. Joseph Arnold saw Glover in the wagon as it passed on the corner of Huron Street. He also identified two men, Brigham and Mosier, as being in the wagon. Henry Clarke, the barber who had been a member of the committee of colored abolitionists, testified later that he had ridden in front of the wagon until it passed him at the corner of Oneida Street, whence he followed it all the way down East Water Street until it crossed the bridge over the Milwaukee River at Walker's Point.[40] F. J. Blair had the impression of "more than one darky" in the wagon and said that it "seemed pretty full."[41] There were a number of observers who reported seeing various colored people in the vicinity of the rescue scene, including one who was identified as being among the group of citizens who had arrived by steamboat from Racine. One witness saw several men run up to the carriage and shake hands with the colored man in the wagon. He heard the Negro in the wagon say to one, "When did you come up from Racine?" indicating Glover recognized a supporter or former acquaintance from Racine.[42]

An additional concern of a number of observers was Sherman Booth's relative proximity to the wagon during the rescue ride. As with so many other aspects of this situation, the estimates of his distance from the wagon varied with the sympathies of the witnesses.

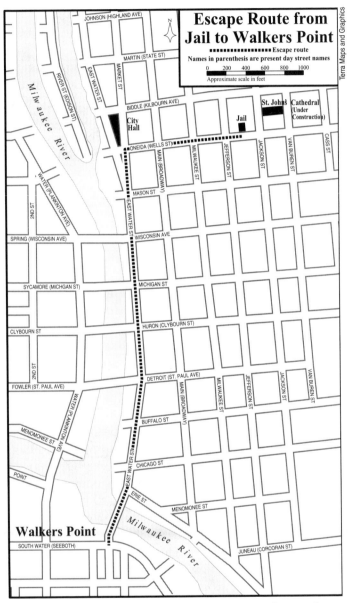

The route followed by Glover and his supporters as they made their way from the jail to Walkers Point.

Those opposed to Glover's release reported having seen Booth riding alongside of it, while those in favor said they did not see him anywhere in the vicinity, or else at a considerable distance. These observations became of some importance at Booth's trial the following year.

At Walker's Point Bridge, Glover got out of the two-horse wagon that had brought him from the jail and was transferred to a lighter, faster buggy pulled by a bobtailed bay. The rig was driven by John Messenger who, having gotten caught up in the drama, offered to help Glover on his next leg of the Underground Railroad to Waukesha. It is not clear from the accounts, however, whether Messenger just happened by. At the time James Angove was getting the battering ram, he had also been told that Messenger's horse had been seen tethered to the fence that surrounded the courthouse, leading to some speculation regarding whether Messenger just happened on the scene at Walker's Point Bridge.

As Glover was transferred from the two-horse wagon to Messenger's buggy, a witness heard someone tell Glover not to be afraid. Caught up by optimism, he replied, "Oh, I'm not afraid, not at all." Just after this exchange, Booth was heard to approve of Messenger's offer, when he said of him, "Yes! Let him go with him, he's a man I can rely upon." This witness, a local factory owner and leader of the local militia named John Jennings, was called by the prosecution to tell his recollections to the court. Jennings had, in fact, been asked to call out the company for crowd control at the jail, but he delayed until he had assurances that his men would be paid by the city.[43]

About ten o'clock Sunday morning, following Saturday's rescue, a group of men gathered at Henry Clarke's Pioneer Hair Salon. Among those present, in addition to Clarke himself, was Booth, whose desire that Glover not be held in jail over the Sabbath had been realized. Also at the shop were a man named Boyd; Avery Hill, who may have been a mason; a Mr. Williams, who had been a hardware store proprietor; an unnamed railroad conductor; and possibly several others who, like Boyd, having seen Booth enter, desired to be brought up to date on the most important event that had happened in recent memory. The topic of conversation was, of course, the previous day's dramatic rescue, as well as

Clark George H., barbering, 22½ Spring, h cor Main and Division

GEORGE H. CLARK,
PIONEER HAIR DRESSING SALOON,

Spring Street, Third door East from American House.

————o————

SHAVING, HAIR CUTTING, SHAMPOONING.

Following the rescue of Joshua Glover, several abolitionists gathered at Henry Clarke's barbershop. This ad, misspelling Clarke's name among other words, appeared in a Milwaukee City Directory of the time.

preparation for the legal action that would most certainly follow shortly. Boyd heard Booth say to Hill, "If you know anything, don't tell it, keep still." Booth then laughed and said, "I don't know anything about it—I wasn't there." Hill said he had gone in the barber shop to get information from Booth but that Booth had said "that he didn't know anything about it, that there didn't anybody know anything about it."[44] Booth's denials were made, of course, with the knowledge that he might later be called to account for his involvement in the affair—an assumption that proved to be true.

While this meeting was taking place, Glover was well on his way to a series of safe houses on the UGRR that would frustrate and eventually baffle the efforts of his erstwhile captors to return him to Missouri.

7

Glover Goes by Rail

As Messenger and his passenger rocketed west on their way to Waukesha, the pounding of their hearts in their ears accompanied the sounds of the horse's labored breathing and the wind whipping past the wagon. As the distance widened between them and any likely pursuers, each was able to turn his thoughts to concerns about how the journey would end.

Until the evening of the rescue, John Messenger had been a person with no known activist record, who had been described by an observer as "a rabid Democrat, changed in a night into a rank abolitionist."[1] Here he was, in the dark of a late winter's night, temperature close to freezing, risking his own freedom, his income as a noted building contractor, the comfort of his wife and children, his life in a home with domestic help, and a good bit of money in order to carry a fugitive slave to the sanctuary of an Underground Railroad station.[2]

The "freight" Messenger was carrying was undoubtedly as confused and frightened as he himself. Until just about two years earlier, Joshua Glover's life had been the ordered and predictable one of a slave whose every action was dictated by the wishes of his master. One of the conditions making such a life unendurable was the total absence of a moment of the day or night that he could call his own. A working man who was not a slave might labor for twelve hours a day, six days a week, but when he left his workplace, he was generally not answerable to his employer. A slave could be called on by his master for some task at three o'clock in the morning as easily as at three o'clock in the afternoon. Now, after two years of freedom; barely a day after a harrowing capture, imprisonment, and escape; still aching from his wounds; and uncertain whether he was being carried to safety or to yet another capture and return to slavery, he was being bounced at high speed along a rutted road through heavily forested land to Waukesha, a town sixteen miles distant, known by the Democrats as "that abolitionist hole."[3]

Before it had that title, Waukesha had existed for about sixteen years as the growing village of Prairieville in the wilds west of Milwaukee. Settled initially by people from western New York and New England, it had previously been the hunting and fishing grounds of numerous Native American tribes. Early white settlers found burial mounds, some dating back many hundreds of years. A contemporary visitor to Waukesha could hardly begin to imagine the area that Messenger and Glover were rapidly approaching or the people they would shortly encounter. The words of the pioneer settlers, some of whom would be enlisted to aid Glover, can, however, convey the difficult and often primitive conditions that existed at that time.

One early settler, Chauncey C. Olin, arrived there in 1836 from upper New York state and described in a letter how he had "traveled a large share of the way from Michigan City to Chicago on the beach of the lake, sometimes in the water up to the depth of two feet to avoid deep sand that had been thrown up by the waves." He continued, "We were now eighteen days from home and had passed what is now Waukegan, Kenosha [then Southport], Racine and the mouth of the Milwaukee River. . . . After resting a few days . . . we took our departure for what was then called Prairie Village, sixteen miles west, through a heavy-timbered country for the first twelve miles."[4]

Another pioneer settler, Lyman Goodnow, arrived a year after Olin. It was he who later escorted Caroline Quarles on her trip to Canada. Having heard glowing reports of the fertility of the land from relatives who had already settled there, Goodnow arrived in Milwaukee by boat in 1837. "I paid 3 cents the next morning to cross the Milwaukee River, and started for Prairieville on foot and alone," he wrote later. "The road was through a heavily timbered country till I passed Poplar Creek where I came to oak openings. . . . I soon came in sight of a small prairie and soon arrived at

Prairieville. . . . I took a job to cut and split 5,000 rails and draw them onto the prairie at $30 per 1,000. I helped Allen Clinton build a neat log house on his place. That winter he and I *borrowed* rails enough of Uncle Sam, to fence his farm."[5]

Vernon Tichenor, Prairieville's first lawyer and an active abolitionist, left his home in Amsterdam, New York, to join his father, who had already purchased land in the new settlement to the west. Traveling by steamboat most of the way, he went from Buffalo to Niagara Falls, New York, then to Erie, Pennsylvania, Cleveland and Sandusky, Ohio, and then on to Detroit, Michigan. Shortly after his arrival, he wrote a letter in early September 1839 to his wife, Charlotte, still in Amsterdam. He said of the people he met in those cities, "The people of Western Pennsylvania, Ohio and Michigan are fierce looking men. They call themselves 'Buckeyes,' 'Wolverines' and 'Hoosiers' and they wear long beards and carry long sharp pointed knives." Next he went up the St. Clair, nearly to Lake Huron, where "some of the passengers went ashore and shot black squirrels, pigeons, hawks, etc. The woods were full of bear and deer. I walked out into the woods without a gun. I could almost walk up to the large hawks. Everything seemed to be unacquainted with man. Their tameness was shocking to me."[6]

Tichenor's next stop was at Mackinac, Michigan, in the middle of the night, chosen as a refueling spot because of its ample supply of firewood and safe harbor. After one more stop, the ship made its way to Milwaukee, where he found his father's family on the point of moving to Prairie Village, at his estimate an eighteen-mile trip. "In a quarter of a mile from the village we entered the forest," Tichenor wrote. "The road is new and only cut through last winter—and very rough. We passed fourteen miles through dense forest, with a few log houses scattered here and there in small clearings. . . . Beyond the forest we went three miles through oak openings and then came to the prairie."[7]

It was the pioneer spirit of those early settlers, as well as their courage, determination in overcoming obstacles to the achievement of their goals, and adherence to their religious principles, that made it possible for them to also carry out their clandestine jobs of escorting fugitive slaves to safety. Just as their histories indicate that they did not always hew to the letter of the law in acquiring property and building material, so did they feel free to break the law when they felt a "higher law" required it.

This adherence to rigid Christian principles was a two-edged sword derived, in part, from the membership of all three settlers in the local Congregational Church, the principles of which they had brought with them from the East. This association not only required them to risk their freedom and fortunes to subvert the laws against resisting slavery, which they regarded as the vilest of evils, but it also mandated that they should treat severely, and with equal vigor, those within their congregation who broke its rules. The founder of the first temperance society in Wisconsin was none other than Lyman Goodnow, the abolitionist.

Among their various efforts to stamp out sin was the occasion when one member of the congregation was speedily excommunicated when he failed to make public reparation for "breaking his covenant by profaning God's holy name and day." Another member who kept horses for hire, on being accused of violating the Sabbath, maintained that because ministers and deacons called for horses on the Sabbath, he could not refuse others. The assembly voted that the charge was sustained by his own admission and he was excommunicated. Yet another member was excommunicated after being charged with "swearing, attending dancing school, and circus."[8]

Not all trials were for sins of the flesh. One deacon, who had absented himself from church for some time because of lack of sympathy with the church's abolitionist position, was charged by the church officials and, refusing to conform to their requirements, demanded a public trial. In the presence of members of other churches, a proslavery lawyer appeared for the defense, and Vernon Tichenor served as prosecutor. The congregant was convicted and excommunicated.[9]

When it came to making moral and ethical choices, these men were little troubled by shades of gray. Something was right or it was wrong, and if it was wrong, it must be made right. These were not principles first learned in Wisconsin. They had learned these precepts from their Christian and abolitionist parents, long before they migrated to the Wisconsin frontier in the mid-1830s in response to an impending federal land sale that encouraged development to the West.

In fact, that imminent land sale, created through a special act of Congress in 1839 and offering land at $1.25 an acre, was to be responsible for one of the great ironies of the struggle between the forces of freedom and those of slavery. Many slaveholders were migrating from the Southeast to the Southwest and the border states, partly because of land depletion as a result of tobacco farming and partly because of the Missouri Compromise of 1820, which opened further lands to slavery. This latest attempt of the federal government to cater to the demands of slaveholders would also make it more difficult for runaway slaves to live safely in the North.

At the same time this was happening, the federal government had also opened for sale portions of the Northwest Territories to encourage settlement and development of the West. This sale, to take place in February 1839, had the unintended additional consequence of populating the area with avid abolitionists from New York and New England, without whose aid Joshua Glover and many other runaways from their Missouri masters would have had a much more difficult time remaining safely in the states or making their way eventually to Canada.

As Messenger approached the outskirts of the village, he began looking for the home of Winchel D. Bacon, to which he had been given directions before leaving Milwaukee. When he had located it, he quietly drew the wagon and its exhausted horse into the shadows near the dwelling. After carefully helping Glover into the house and examining and cleaning his wounds, Bacon decided Glover would need to stay a while to recover, both from the wounds and from the rigors of his journey. Bacon also thought that in his present condition it would not be safe to quarter Glover in the village. He then consulted with his friends, Vernon Tichenor; Dr. W. D. Holbrook, a dentist; and Bacon's brother-in-law, Charles Blackwell. The group decided to move Glover to the farm of Moses Tichenor, Vernon's father. Traveling across the fields in the mud and darkness, Vernon made his way to his father's farm, about two miles south of the village. Arousing his father from sleep, Vernon asked his permission to hide Glover on his property, and the senior

Tichenor at once consented. Vernon then returned to Bacon's home, collected Glover, and once again set out for the farm. On arriving there, he saw several people in the dim light at the farmhouse, and he drew back, thinking he had been followed. A closer look revealed Bacon and Holbrook, who had trailed them silently to make sure Glover was not captured.[10]

While Glover remained hidden in Moses Tichenor's barn, C. C. Olin, who had been appointed by the group to be Glover's conductor on the next stage of the journey, made arrangements to escort him to Racine, the abolitionists probably believing the slave catchers would not anticipate it as a departure point for Canada, because Glover had so recently been captured there. In addition to his active role in the church, Olin was also a singer and orator of note, as well as being editor of the local abolitionist newspaper, the *Waukesha Freeman*. He, too, stood to lose much if he was apprehended by the law while conducting Glover to safety.

Olin planned to take Glover through Muskego and then to Racine by way of the plank road from Rochester. At that time of year, the roads were in very rough condition, and travel times were slower than they would be later in the year. Added to that was the need to stay off the more heavily traveled routes and, when possible, to travel protected by the cover of darkness. The pair traveled in a reasonably direct manner to Muskego Center where they picked up the Milwaukee and Janesville Plank Road and from there on, in the words of C. C. Olin, "We found good sail as we had struck the plank road."[11]

He had a fleet team, and about three hours after leaving Waukesha, Olin was at the door of Richard E. Ela of Rochester, some twenty miles from his starting point. Knocking at the door, he called out, "Hello." "Who's there?" came the reply from within. "A friend of a friend," responded Olin, using the code language to designate an abolitionist with a "package." "It's C. C. Olin from Waukesha." Opening the door, Ela asked, "Well, what has called you here at this time of night?" Olin replied, "I have a premium load. I have a colored man by the name of Joshua Glover."[12]

At this point in his handwritten narrative, prepared about thirty-five years after the event, Olin has himself making a speech to Ela about the capture and rescue of Glover. The oration is filled with the florid phrases of the mid-nineteenth-century, language that was common when abolitionists decried the evils of the Fugitive Slave Law and its supporters. Whether Olin did, in fact, deliver this speech to Ela while standing outside his home late on a cold night in March 1854 may be less important than the fact that such utterances truly reflected both his feelings and his dedication to the task of uprooting slavery in this country. It was for him as sacred a trust as rooting out sinners in the congregation.

Olin went on to say, "Now sir, I want your team. As you can see, mine look a little jaded as we have been out a little over three hours coming from Waukesha." Ela responded by offering a team, adding, "and here is five dollars to go with it." Calling into the house, Ela requested that tea be prepared and that his farmhand hitch a team to Olin's wagon.[13]

Glover was then taken into the house for refreshments and so both Ela and his wife, Nancy, could get a good look at him. As they were eating, conversation may have revealed that this was Ela's second marriage, his first wife having died within six months of their wedding. It may have also been learned that, in addition to being a mechanic, Ela, who was not yet forty, operated a fanning mill with the assistance of a number of employees who lived on his property. Here, indeed, was yet another hardworking pioneer who had much to lose if his clandestine occupation became known.[14]

When the meal was concluded, the travelers, after thanking their hosts, climbed back in the wagon and continued their journey over the final twenty miles. "We met with no resistance on our way and about 7 o'clock a.m. I deposited Joshua Glover at the house of the Rev. Mr. A. P. *[sic]* Kinney, a Cong. Minister. There he was protected by the good people of Racine until some safer means could be provided to send him to Canada."[15]

The clergyman's residence, located at the corner of Liberty and Marquette Streets, was about three blocks from his church. Both buildings were also within a block or two of the Root River in a neighborhood that came to be known as "a nest of churches," because there were no fewer than ten houses of worship within a few square blocks.[16] This location, being as close to the harbor as it was, would also allow for Glover to be escorted quickly to a ship if necessary.

Glover's Underground Railroad Route

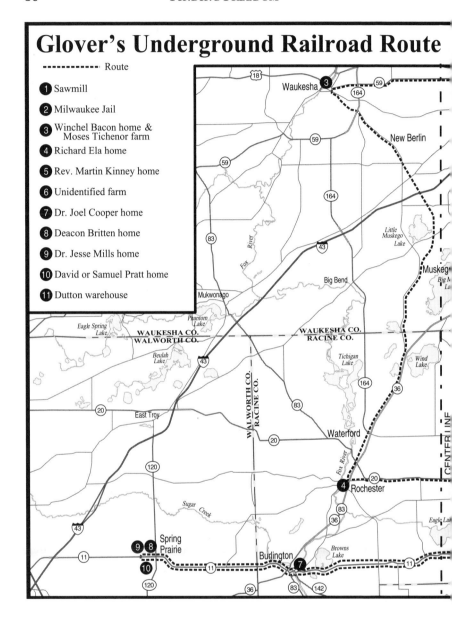

- - - - - - - - - - Route

1 Sawmill

2 Milwaukee Jail

3 Winchel Bacon home & Moses Tichenor farm

4 Richard Ela home

5 Rev. Martin Kinney home

6 Unidentified farm

7 Dr. Joel Cooper home

8 Deacon Britten home

9 Dr. Jesse Mills home

10 David or Samuel Pratt home

11 Dutton warehouse

The Reverend Martin Palmer Kinney was a man of many facets. While still living in upstate New York, he studied for the law, which he continued to do for a while after arriving in Wisconsin at the law firm of Finch and Lynn. Eventually, he felt the call of the church and was ordained in the Congregational Church in 1844. Before being assigned to the Racine church in 1852 as its first pastor, he served in Kenosha and Whitewater. As was true of many of the educated men in the community, he did not limit himself to his primary job, in this instance, the pastorate of his church. He was also the clerk of the general convention of his church and served as superintendent of schools in Racine.[17]

It is not known how long the Reverend Kinney harbored Glover and whether he kept Glover in his home or hidden in the church, but it turns out to have been a good idea to have moved him from Waukesha to Racine. "Abolitionist hole" that it might have been, Waukesha also had its complement of proslavery advocates. Within a day or two of Glover's return to Racine, Sherman Booth was hung in effigy in Waukesha.[18]

Even though Benammi Garland was now safely back in St. Louis, where he was busy filing civil lawsuits against his adversaries in Wisconsin, it was still considered unsafe to keep Glover in one place for very long. There were too many who were eager to collect the reward Garland would undoubtedly pay for Glover's apprehension. For this reason, Glover was shuttled for the next few weeks through several UGRR stations in Racine and Walworth Counties. After he left the Reverend Kinney's, he was reported to have spent a brief time at the home of a farmer outside Racine.[19]

While it is not certain by what form of transportation he journeyed to that farmer's home, or to his next stop, there is some existing evidence how the move may have been accomplished. Susan Payne Clement, born in 1851, was the daughter of Alfred Payne, a tollgate keeper on a road in Racine County. She also identified him in an unpublished reminiscence, written late in her life, as "one of the hated abolitionists." In her memoir she reports a story told to her when she was a child: ". . . and one night a wagon came from Racine, through the tollgate, which my father was for some reason expecting. It was midnight, very dark and quiet except for the tramp of the two horses and two men were on the load of hay. A few quiet words, the tollgate was opened, the load went through and the gate was again closed and locked. The wagon promptly passed on its way, and its contents, a negro runaway slave, put off safely to Canada. He was hidden in the bottom of the wagon, under a load of hay built up on a false bottom above him. I think the negro's name was Glover."[20]

The writer goes on to state that when she married, she acquired as a father-in-law one Charles Clement. This is the same Charles Clement who was the editor of the *Racine Advocate* at the time of Glover's capture. She also identifies him as being the leader of the party that broke Glover out of the Racine jail and put him under the load of hay.[21]

While she had some of her facts wrong, in that Clement was in Milwaukee at the time Glover was broken out of *that* jail, she correctly identified Clement's sympathies. She also described a vehicle of a type that has figured in other accounts of fugitive slave transport on the UGRR in general, as well as in southeastern Wisconsin. In Bristol, located in Kenosha County, the Kellogg Tavern was reputed to be a stop on the UGRR. Theodore Fellows, whose father owned a farm in Genoa City, near the Illinois border, recollects that when he was about sixteen, he drove a wagon, similar to the one described earlier, from his father's farm to the tavern, where he unwittingly saw a fugitive slave who had been hidden in a compartment under the grain stored above him.[22]

Glover's departure from the unidentified farm was his next-to-the-last exit from Racine County. He was then brought to the home of Dr. Joel H. Cooper in Burlington. A physician and pharmacist, Dr. Cooper had moved with his wife to Burlington from Spring Prairie in 1851, following the birth of their first child, Henry, a year earlier. The home that the Coopers selected for their residence was probably chosen for more than its attractive appearance. It had been built about fifteen years earlier. In addition to having a stair rail and newel post of solid black walnut, which had been brought by oxcart from New York, and floors of solid maple and walnut, as well as walls two feet thick, it also contained a room under the kitchen that was used to hide runaway slaves. The home had been built originally by Silas Peck, who had also hidden slaves there.[23]

Dr. Cooper was a neighbor of Dr. Edward G. Dyer, another abolitionist of note. In 1842, Dyer had been instrumental in collecting money for the fugitive slave Caroline Quarles, who was passing through Burlington on her way to Canada. Dyer was also the founder of the Burlington Liberty Association, one of many forerunners of the Republican Party.[24] In addition to providing a forum to discuss its political agenda, the association's gatherings also served as a common meeting ground for abolitionists in a setting where their words would not be leaked to others.

On July 4, 1840, two years before he rendered assistance to Caroline Quarles, Dyer was selected by the citizens of the area to deliver the first Independence Day oration held at Delavan, in Walworth County. His speech covered a wide range of topics in the history of the country, with a large portion of it devoted to a vigorous denunciation of the evils of slavery, including emphasis on the concept that all men are created free and equal.

As Dyer reached the conclusion of his speech, he praised the manner in which the current settlers of the territory had improved conditions over those that had existed before their arrival, when the indigenous people had dominated the landscape, saying the country at that time "presented nothing but signs of savage wanderers, amidst native wilds, checkered by Indian trails, and traversed by Indian hunters, now teeming with civilized life and animated by healthful, vigorous and well directed enterprise." He continued:

> To the lonely traveler, who may have been a visitor here and a discoverer of the verdant prairies and beautiful groves that surround us; what a soul-cheering contrast would this day afford. Instead of Indian wigwams may be seen comfortable habitations, tenanted with intelligent, enterprising and refined citizens. Instead of groups of painted savages, decorated in Indian costume and armed in deadly strife, may be witnessed, respectable and cultivated social circles, clad in the habiliments of neatness and peace. Instead of the terrific war whoop and savage revellings of a barbarous and untutored race, may this day be heard, the triumphal rejoicings of the arts over ignorance, of science over bigotry, of liberty over despotism.[25]

It appears that Dr. Dyer, as well as a number of others opposed to slavery either in its entirety or in its extension into the western territories, had some difficulty including under the umbrella of liberty those groups whose style of existence threatened the primacy of the free-enterprise system.

It is no surprise that Glover's next stop on the UGRR was Spring Prairie, just west of the Racine County line, in Walworth County. Cooper's former residence there had undoubtedly acquainted him with a number of abolitionist sympathizers. Glover is said to have stayed first at the residence of Deacon Britten.[26] While there, he was observed to still be wearing a bandage on his head and had been on the move for at least two weeks. During that time this wounded and travel-worn fugitive had been hauled around the countryside a total of more than one hundred miles, while presently being little more than twenty miles from the site of his capture in Racine. He was due for yet more travel and more hospitality from strangers before his journey would safely end.

Following his sojourn with Deacon Britten, Glover was conveyed to the home of Dr. Jesse Mills and his wife, Mary, in the town of Lafayette. Mary Ann Bell, the teenage niece of Mrs. Mills, was living with the family following her mother's death. One night, she and her cousin, who were sharing a bedroom, were awakened by noises and were frightened to hear footsteps in the little-used room above them. The next morning, the younger girl saw her aunt at the head of the stairs with something in her hand that was covered by an apron. She told her cousin that Aunt Mary was serving somebody breakfast. Curiosity getting the better of them, she crept up the stairs while the other girl watched. She then rapped on the door as she had seen her aunt do. The door was opened cautiously, and the girl suddenly came down the stairs, rolling in her terror and haste. When her cousin asked what she had seen, she replied, "The biggest blackest nigger in the world."[27]

They avoided the stairway for the rest of the day. Late that night they heard steps on the stairs and subdued voices outside their door; then they heard the creaking of wheels going down the lane. They never spoke of the incident to their elders. It wasn't until years later that they learned they had frightened Joshua Glover as much as he had them.[28]

Young Mary Bell eventually became the wife of Walter Derthick, whose family had moved to a property adjoining Dr. Mills when Walter was fifteen, in the same year that Mary had encountered Joshua Glover. Many years later, Mrs. Derthick contributed the story of her encounter with Glover to the author of a history of Walworth County.

The next stop for Glover was said to be at the home of David Pratt, also in Walworth County, although Sherman Booth, almost fifty years after the event, in a letter to Richard Ela's daughter, Ida, identified David's brother, Samuel, as the one who sheltered Glover.[29] Over the course of the several weeks that had passed since Glover's rescue, no fewer than nine abolitionists, plus their family members, had fed, clothed, and sheltered Joshua Glover while moving him, at great risk to themselves, around an area of the countryside encompassing four counties. This heroic effort allowed his rescuers to set him on a maritime journey that would bring him across hundreds of miles of inland sea to the safety and freedom of the Queen's realm.

At about this time, the attentions of the proslavery elements were focused on the legal events taking place in Milwaukee, where Sherman Booth and other abolitionists were defending themselves against charges of violating the provisions of the Fugitive Slave Act. Glover was fairly well recovered from his wounds. This made it a propitious time to prepare for the final stage of his journey to freedom. Secrecy and careful planning had, up to this point, made it possible to move him undetected through about a half dozen stations of the UGRR. Even though Racine was thought to be a relatively safe hiding place for a brief time, absolute caution and discretion were necessary to ensure that he was placed safely aboard a ship that would deliver him to Canada. For this task, no more qualified person could be found than A. P. Dutton.

Born to a farming family in upstate New York in 1822, Achas Perry Dutton, known to his friends as Perry, shared the entrepreneurial spirit of so many of the early pioneers who later became abolitionists. About 1834, when he was twelve, he and his parents left New York for Huron, Ohio. He left that home at nineteen, arriving in Racine in 1841. Within a few years of his arrival, he had been a partner in three shipping and forwarding firms, opened a hotel, and owned an interest in several vessels.[30]

Racine Heritage Museum Archives

The Dutton Warehouse in Racine Harbor, c. 1857: Glover's final refuge in Wisconsin before crossing Lake Michigan to freedom in Canada.

Around this time, Racine was fifth on the western lakes in vessel tonnage, exceeding Milwaukee and exceeded only by Buffalo, Cleveland, Detroit, and Chicago.[31] Among his other accomplishments, Dutton was one of the promoters of the first telegraph line between Chicago and Milwaukee, an undertaking that Joshua Glover could be grateful for, because it was that instrument that allowed news of his capture in Racine to arrive quickly in Milwaukee. He also built Racine's first piers and elevator, making a market for the grain that was a chief source of income for the early settlers.[32] In 1843, before Racine had a deep harbor, Dutton would go out in a scow to unload passengers and their luggage for the trip to shore.[33] By 1846, he was the agent for thirteen shipping lines whose craft called at Racine.[34] By 1852, when Glover arrived in town, the firm of Dutton and Raymond handled as much as a million bushels of grain annually, in addition to other commodities.[35]

As with so many businessmen of that time, Dutton operated more on the basis of confidence in the future than on the amount of money in his pocket. In an 1899 letter to the editor of the local paper, Dutton revealed one method by which business was done in the 1840s that would leave many of today's entrepreneurs green with envy. "I have been thinking over old times and how business was done, when I borrowed hundreds of thousands of dollars with which to buy grain, pork and wool. I would give a note for $5000 for instance, payable at some bank in New York sixty days after date. The bank would discount the note and credit me with the amount less 12%, which he took in advance. So I got but $4900 [*sic*]. Now, when the notes became due, New York exchange was scarce and I paid from one-half to 2% exchange, and yet the note laid in the vault at Racine all of the time and no one in New York ever saw the note."[36]

Dutton's views on temperance seemed less extreme than those of his fellow abolitionists. He handled whisky as one of his cargoes, and there was found in his scrapbook a prescription for horse distemper that contained two quarts of whiskey to a half pint of other ingredients, including belladonna and sulfuric acid.[37]

Noted though he was as an important businessman of this growing town, Dutton's interests were not confined to forwarding grain and butter, nor to the racing of fast horses, an interest he shared with J. I. Case, the owner of a prosperous threshing machine business. The warehouse of Dutton and Raymond was also a station on the UGRR and was used as Glover's last hiding place in Wisconsin. In his later years, Dutton wrote in a letter to Wilbur Siebert, author of the early, definitive book *The Underground Railroad from Slavery to Freedom*, that more than one hundred fugitive slaves had embarked from Racine's harbor to Canada.[38] While this could have been something of an exaggeration brought on by age and time, it still indicates considerable abolitionist activity in Racine.

The final hurdle that Glover had to clear before freedom would be in his grasp involved an experience he had never encountered in the forty years he had been alive. That was the arduous journey across the Great Lakes from Racine to Canada. The hundreds of ships plying the waters of this great inland sea, not yet having been supplanted by the railroads, were still the largest movers of goods and passengers between Chicago and the East Coast. Fortunately for those fugitive slaves who made it past Chicago to Wisconsin, the western shore of Lake Michigan was dotted with many ports in which a slave could be safely hidden until a friendly captain, bound for Detroit or Buffalo, agreed to add some unlisted freight to his cargo. Those captains, who came from the same part of the Northeast as the abolitionists, probably would not have agreed to take on such passengers if they had not shared the abolitionists' views on the evils of slavery.

Although steam-powered craft had been in service on the nation's waterways for most of the nineteenth century, their use on the Great Lakes was not without hazard. Of the 199 steamships on the lakes in the thirty-five years between 1818 and 1853, 27 percent were wrecked, burned, or exploded.[39] If more than one in four of today's common modes of transportation wrecked, sank, or fell from the sky, few companies would trust their cargo to them, and even fewer passengers would use them. The opportunity to move one's goods, or oneself, from Milwaukee to Buffalo in three to four days, as opposed to overland travel taking up to several weeks, was so desirable that if it didn't overcome fear, it was at least possible to suppress it long enough to make the journey and then enjoy the advantages that speed brought, even then. Living in those times was a more hazardous enterprise than can be easily appreciated in this era.

To complicate the situation further, a number of those ships, even though not involved in accidents, still encountered fog, ice, and storms. In 1848, one of the proudest vessels on the Great Lakes, the steamer *Sultana*, its 30-feet-high paddle wheel propelling its 250-feet length through the waters of Lake Michigan, was driven onto the rocks three miles north of Racine. After several hours, during which her large number of passengers were at risk, she was pulled off by tugs, with no permanent damage, and proceeded on her journey.[40] At about the same time that near tragedy was being averted, another ship, the steamer *America*, was arriving safely at Milwaukee with seventy tons of freight and nearly three hundred people, the greatest number of cabin passengers ever brought up the lakes.[41]

Two years later, in early April of 1850, the same *Sultana* that had been on the rocks off Racine, after making it easily from Buffalo to Detroit, set off up the lake for the journey through the straits of Mackinac to Milwaukee. Encountering ice in the straits, she was held up for thirty hours before she could continue on her way.[42]

No record was found naming the ship on which Glover embarked for Canada, although several captains who stopped regularly at Racine were noted for being willing to take the risk of transporting fugitive slaves to Canada. Although the date he left is not precisely known, it is likely that he took ship for Canada in the first two weeks of April 1854. It is also likely that he traveled north, through the straits of Mackinac, then to Georgian Bay, and disembarked at Owen Sound or Collingwood. He most certainly would not have been lodged in one of the passenger cabins on the main deck. While he may have been in steerage with the majority of the passengers, he was more likely put aboard at night and concealed amid the cargo, in an uncomfortable but safe place, where discovery by anyone unfriendly to the cause was less likely to occur. While the journey, under the best conditions, might take only three days or so, it could not in any sense be called comfortable. Food would have been sneaked to him, and there would have been no toilet facilities other than a pail delivered to him and removed by the captain or a trusted crewman. Glover would have needed to remain in a cramped position for most of the journey, except for some surreptitious stretching late at night, when the other passengers were asleep.

It is quite likely, regardless of the discomfort that he would suffer over the next few days, that the feeling that ran through Glover when he felt the engine vibrations through his feet and heard the paddle wheels biting into the water and the timbers creaking with the gathering speed of the boat was one of relief at finally getting beyond the reach of both Benammi Garland and the Fugitive Slave Law. He had but a few days to wait before he set foot on Canadian soil and would once again be able to cry out "Hallelujah," as he had been heard to do when he was rescued from jail more than five weeks earlier, many hundreds of miles away.

8

Trials and Tribulations

The events involving the capture and rescue of Glover, which led to the trials of his rescuers, demonstrate the multiple facets of abolitionists' positions. Joshua Glover, Sherman Booth, John Messenger, and John Rycraft were all abolitionists, each for his own reasons—not always identical but sometimes converging. Glover's reasons were, of course, highly personal. The reasons of the others were often moral, political, and/or philosophical, as well as personal. Such variety of reasons made it possible for Booth to say, when he addressed the crowd at the courthouse square, "It was not merely for the sake of the imprisoned Glover, within these walls, that this vast assemblage has met; for he is comparatively insignificant, and, until today, his very existence was unknown to us."[1]

Although Glover and others in his situation may have been disappointed by Booth's sentiments, they would not have been surprised. Glover certainly would have approved of the methods used on his behalf.

Joshua Glover was but one of many thousands of fugitive slaves who made their way to Canada on the Underground Railroad. In this instance, however, there was much more involved than the act of one slave stealing himself from his owner. The time at which he did it, the manner in which it was accomplished, the particular individuals and groups involved on both sides of the incident, and the overall consequences all served as elements contributing to momentous political and judicial upheaval in a country barely seventy-five years old and a state that had been a part of the Northwest Territory only seven years earlier.

As a direct result of this event, the Republican Party was hastened into existence, producing Abraham Lincoln as its first president. The doctrine of nullification, which held that any state could suspend within its boundaries the operation or implementation of any federal law it deemed to be unconstitutional, was used by Wisconsin years before it was invoked by South Carolina, and the bloody conflict of the Civil War was brought closer. The effects spread far beyond the borders of Wisconsin, first to Boston, during the celebrated trial of a runaway slave named Anthony Burns in June of the same year, where Byron Paine's pamphlet, "Unconstitutionality of the Fugitive Slave Act," was required reading for every abolitionist; then to New York, where abolitionists, heartened by the success in Wisconsin, wrote laudatory letters to Paine; and to the nation's capital, where Chief Justice Taney, in 1858, declared the Wisconsin Supreme Court to be in rebellion and demanded it reverse its decision that the Fugitive Slave Law was unconstitutional.[2]

While in one sense, the rescue of Joshua Glover was a catalyst, the people taking part in it were elements of the reaction. The lives of most of the major actors were changed in ways they could never have imagined.

While writs of habeas corpus, requiring that the government show cause why a prisoner should be held, may have been denied to captured fugitive slaves, their use among activists, both pro- and antislavery, was common. Following the rescue of Glover, writs, affidavits, motions, indictments, interrogatories, criminal trials, and civil suits traveled among courts in St. Louis, Madison, Racine, and Milwaukee as rapidly as telegraph, ship, rail, and horse could carry them. The trials that flowed from this stream of legal process were to occupy some of the participants in this drama for almost seven years, enriching some, imprisoning and impoverishing others, and in one case, probably resulting in a premature death.

The first of these actions began within hours of Glover's rescue when Charles Clement, the editor of the *Racine Advocate*, signed a complaint seeking the arrest of B. S. Garland and others for the assault of Joshua Glover.[3] Garland was promptly arrested by Sheriff Timothy Morris of Racine. Garland immediately responded with a writ of habeas corpus requiring his accusers to appear in federal court and show cause why he should not be released. He was subsequently freed and returned with all speed to St. Louis.[4]

From that city, Garland launched a series of civil suits designed to help him recover the damages he believed were inflicted on him by the loss of his valuable property. Within two weeks of his return, he filed suits seeking two thousand dollars from each of several people for the loss of Joshua Glover.[5] His use of legal process in this instance was reminiscent of the ways he used the Missouri courts, more than a decade earlier, in an effort to procure money then owed to him. In both instances, his behavior could be described only as unrelenting.

It might have been expected that Garland would sue Booth, Messenger, and Rycraft early on, because he knew they would also be criminally tried and were likely to be convicted, making financial recovery even more likely. Not content with suits that had merit under the law, in December 1854 he even filed suit against U.S. Marshal Stephen V. Abelman, alleging the negligence of his deputy, Marshal C. C. Cotton, from whose custody Glover was rescued.[6] This was not the first time that Cotton had encountered the law from the other side of the bar. In 1853 he spent a brief time in jail on a contempt citation from a county judge for refusing to respond speedily to a writ of habeas corpus for a prisoner he had in federal custody.[7]

While the trials of Sherman Booth were the most time-consuming and have received the greatest coverage, the most poignant outcome of the Glover affair is reserved for John A. Messenger, that apparently instant convert to abolition's cause, who conveyed Glover to Waukesha.

Born in Berkshire County, Massachusetts, in 1810, Messenger moved to Milwaukee in 1836. He had previously studied for medicine but entered real estate upon arriving in Milwaukee, where he made considerable progress as a contractor for public buildings and private homes.[8] Regarded as one of the pioneer settlers, he had owned a brickyard as early as 1844.[9] Later he had won a contract to build a half dozen Milwaukee schools.[10] Two months before Glover's rescue, Messenger had been elected vice president of the Milwaukee Fireman's Association, a testimonial to his standing among the volunteer fire brigades.[11]

The only image of Joshua Glover known to exist, this hand-drawn portrait by C. C. Olin may not be entirely realistic.

Messenger had a reputation as a generous, impulsive, warm-hearted man.[12] These character traits may have been the ones operating when he agreed to convey Glover to Waukesha. From the time of that daring and completely unpredictable journey with Glover, his whole world was turned on its ear. Shortly after he had completed the journey, and before returning to Milwaukee, Mes-

A. P. Dutton, businessman who provided Glover's last stop on the UGRR.

Sherman Booth, newspaper editor who orchestrated Glover's rescue.

Byron Paine, Sherman Booth's attorney and later a Wisconsin Supreme Court Justice.

Thomas Watson, Milwaukee citizen and outspoken opponent of slavery.

senger was reportedly overwhelmed with anxiety.[13] He began to contemplate the consequences to him of his rash act. Fearful of discovery if he returned immediately to Milwaukee, he decided to drive to Racine, where he had friends with whom he could remain overnight, while he contemplated his next steps. His horse being spent from the speedy trip, he probably acquired one for his return. His friends, when he arrived, were alarmed by his strange actions.

Courtesy of Lynchburg Museum System

Benammi Stone Garland, Missouri slave owner who purchased Glover in 1850.

WHi Image ID 2834. R. A. Clifford, Wisconsin Historical Society Museum

Andrew G. Miller, Federal District Court judge who presided over abolitionists' trials.

Courtesy of Milwaukee County Historical Society

Jonathan Arnold, attorney for Benammi S. Garland.

Messenger, who was ordinarily lighthearted and jovial, was on that night gloomy and silent. He paced the floor all night and refused to eat and drink.[14]

In early April, Messenger was served by Garland with a civil suit for two thousand dollars for aiding in the escape of Glover.[15] In early July, along with Booth and Rycraft, Messenger was indicted on the criminal charges of having aided a fugitive slave.[16] On Wednesday, August 2, he was arrested and given bail to appear in court. Surety was supplied by another prominent Milwaukee citizen, William Whitnall.[17]

Two days later, Messenger was dead. In the newspaper of Saturday, August 5, his death of the previous day was reported, with no indication of its cause and the further announcement that his funeral would take place that afternoon.[18] No obituary appeared in the paper, but on September 2 the Milwaukee Fire Association published a resolution of sympathy to the widow and family of John Messenger.[19] On September 11, 1854, his attorney appeared before the federal district court to inform it of Messenger's death, whereupon the court abated the civil suit.[20]

No certificate citing a cause of death has been located. The closeness of Messenger's death to his arrest, coupled with the speed of his funeral and the absence of an obituary, strongly suggest a death from other than so-called natural causes. His death was said by his friends to have been hastened by his mental suffering, if not precipitated by his fear of the consequences.[21] Whatever the cause, John Messenger was one more casualty in the war against slavery.

Following the July indictment, Rycraft was tried and convicted of assisting in the rescue of Glover. Such news undoubtedly had done little to advance Messenger's peace of mind. If his death could have been postponed a few months, he would have learned there were difficulties with the indictments that had been handed down in Madison.

Throughout the fall and winter of 1854, lawyers for the defendants fought vigorously to have the indictments quashed. One of the parties in this effort was Charles Watkins, who, as an attorney, had visited Glover in jail and found himself arrested for his efforts in behalf of habeas corpus. Although he was not a central figure in the affair, his comments to Court Commissioner Winfield Smith represent an excellent example of the tensions existing in the arena of freedom versus slavery. Watkins said:

If it be an offense that I visited a man in prison, then I am guilty. If it be a crime to sympathize with those who are in affliction, then I am not ambitious to appear altogether innocent. It is true that when sent for, I visited a man in prison. It is true when the prisoner told me that he had been knocked down with clubs, bound in chains and dragged in an inclement night, without covering upon his head, and with scarce any clothing upon his person, to a distant jail, I did not approve of the act. It is true that when I saw the stains of blood from his bleeding wounds, I was not wholly insensible to his sufferings and wrong. But that I told him he could have a fair trial by Jury or that his case would be heard by an impartial Court, I deny. His complexion forbid the one, and I should have been false to my convictions if I had given him any assurance of the other. The only consolation I did or could give him was his right to the writ of habeas corpus, and I explained to him that such writ was a writ of right, a writ that the fugitive slave act had not taken away and the only right that was left to a man of his complexion under his accusation. . . . The benefits of this I vouchsafed to secure to him. It was applied for against the Sheriff who *actually* held him under restraint, and the writ was defeated by the return in fiction of law that he was in the *legal* custody of the Marshal. Another writ was applied for and served upon the Marshal. To this, according to local precedent, there was open and avowed disobedience, and the prisoner, disappointed, was without hope. As a last resort, application was made to Judge Miller and though too penurious to be entirely honest, too willful to be ordinarily just, some hope was entertained of clemency from his cowardice, but while the latter did not forsake him, he was not possessed of the former, and he refused any interference, persisting that the Marshal ought not to obey the writ of habeas corpus from a State Court and that he would not then entertain the case himself. . . . Now Mr. Commissioner, to all this I confess, and plead not guilty to the complaint, and shall at all times be ready for trial, and if I am not convicted I shall entertain at no time any suspicion that it is from any fault of the court. . . .[22]

In the following day's edition of the paper, Court Commissioner Smith denied that Watkins had made, in his appearance before him, any uncomplimentary remarks about the judge or the court.[23]

While the court was sitting at Milwaukee for the January 1855 term, Booth's attorneys succeeded in demonstrating that while the indictment had specified that Glover was a slave and did owe service to Garland, it neglected to state that he was a *fugitive* slave and therefore subject to recovery and return. The indictment against Booth, who had not yet been tried, was set aside. Flushed with this victory, Rycraft's lawyers demanded that he, who had already been convicted, not be tried again. They could not make this particular concept of double jeopardy prevail and, much to their dismay, a new grand jury was impaneled in Milwaukee.[24]

While Glover was still being shuttled on the UGRR among various safe houses in southeastern Wisconsin, Booth made his first court appearance. On March 21 he appeared before U.S. Court Commissioner Winfield Smith for a preliminary hearing on a charge of aiding in the rescue of Joshua Glover.[25] This was the first of multiple hearings, indictments, and trials, stretching over many years, during which he would be fined twice, imprisoned three times, "rescued" from jail by friends, and spend thirty-five thousand dollars on his defense. During a ten-month period from March 1, 1860, to January 1, 1861, the office of the U.S. marshal for the district of Wisconsin expended more than thirty-four hundred dollars for the care, feeding, and guarding of him as well as the costs of searching for him following his escape.[26]

Booth shared a characteristic common to many abolitionist activists and entrepreneurs of his day. He was single-minded in his devotion to his cause. Had he not been so before his arrest, he would certainly have become so following it. From the moment he saw Joshua Glover's back disappearing down the road to Waukesha, he was to know no peace for the next seven years. While he was undergoing questioning, waiting for an indictment to be handed down, and being tried for the crime of breaking the Fugitive Slave Law, he continued to actively and vigorously report his own case in his newspaper. Thus we learn from his newspaper, reported in Racine in early July 1854: "Madison is full of people, and the two courts draw a crowd of clients, lawyers and witnesses. The Grand Jury are still sitting on the Glover case and have not yet made their report. One of the Jury, from Iowa, I believe, considers abolitionists as, *prima facie*, thieves and criminals. Twelve such Grand Jurors would indict any Free Soilers on general principles, without proof. We presume they are not all of this stripe."[27]

In spite of the serious nature of the proceedings, there was the occasional light note. The *Racine Advocate* reported the following story from Madison under the title "Barberous Treatment":

> A certain personage residing not a thousand miles from Racine, who assisted in the catching of Glover, the fugitive slave, last spring, recently visited this place, and walking into Noland's dressing saloon, in the basement of the Capitol House, threw off his coat and cravat, and squared himself for the customary tonsorial operation. The proprietor happened to know him and his past history, very politely told him that he did not shave kidnappers or their underlings. The discomforted and hirsute individual was obliged to put on his cast-off garments and decamp.[28]

Apart from the incident perhaps giving the man some small sense of the pain of discrimination, it also raises the possibility that Officer Melvin of the St. Louis police may have been a witness at the grand jury hearings.

While Booth and his attorneys were trying to overthrow the first indictment, preparations were being made for Garland's civil suit to go forward. The Milwaukee attorneys, Arnold and Hamilton, representing Garland in his civil suit, sent a series of eight interrogatories to be answered by three people in St. Louis. These were accompanied by four cross-interrogatories from Booth's attorneys. The persons to be queried were J. P. Garland, who is probably Joseph Parker Garland, the eldest son of Benammi Garland; George Johnson, a physician; and David McCullough, a keeper of a livery stable, who was also the marshal of St. Louis County. The purpose of these questions was for Garland to furnish proof that, at the time of his escape, Joshua Glover was the legal slave of Garland in Missouri, that he fit the description of the man arrested in Racine, and that Garland had lost a substantial investment as a result of his property absconding. Booth's lawyers, James and Byron Paine, took this opportunity to frame their questions as an indictment of slavery and of everyone associated with it.

This proceeding was really just a legal formality, because it was a foregone conclusion that Garland would prevail under the laws of the day. The answers to the questions, however, provide an unusual opportunity to view opinions about slavery through the eyes of two citizens who were not themselves slave owners and to observe their attempts to defend their association with the institution. They also give one of the most complete physical descriptions of Glover available anywhere. For reasons unknown, J. P. Garland apparently was not available to respond to the interrogatories. This may have been because, as the eldest son of B. S. Garland, he would be thought to be biased in favor of his father's position.

After testifying that Glover was a slave of B. S. Garland and that when he left Garland, he was a slave for life, the deponents were then asked about Glover's physical description and value. Marshal McCullough responded that he believed Glover to be between forty-four and forty-five years old in the spring of 1852, about five feet eight to ten inches in height, and rather slender. He described Glover as having long legs for a man of his height; large feet and hands; a heavy, bushy head of hair; eyes rather small and inclined to be red or inflamed, which he believed was probably from hard drinking; complexion brown, not a clear black; and rather stooped shoulders. And he said Glover moved slowly.[29]

Dr. Johnson's description was markedly similar to that of Marshal McCullough, except he reduced Glover's estimated age by a few years and darkened his complexion while still retaining its brown color. He did not remark on the character of his eyes; nor did he say anything about alcohol use.

When the witnesses, who were each questioned separately, a day apart, were faced with the emotionally loaded questions supplied by Booth's attorneys, it became apparent that their answers arrived on their lips with somewhat greater difficulty than their formulaic responses to the previous questions. This was particularly true in the first and fourth questions, which were, in part, "Has it not been your occupation for some part of your life to hunt fugitive slaves for a reward[,] and to enable you the better to hunt them have you not kept bloodhounds trained for that business? . . . What has been your experience in selling men, women and children in that Market? How many men have you sold in St. Louis, how many women and for what purpose, how many children have you weighed off by the pound and separated from their mothers? . . ."[30]

These are not the kinds of questions that gentlemen in slaveholding states were accustomed to being asked, particularly on their home ground, and to have it implied that they were akin to Simon Legree in *Uncle Tom's Cabin* was more than they could comfortably abide. Both deponents declared, with emphasis, that they were not themselves slave owners and never had been. Dr. Johnson went on to say that his knowledge of such matters was derived from his friends and acquaintances who owned slaves and that he had never participated in any of the cruel practices named in the questions. At the same time that he distanced himself from ownership of slaves, he defended the plaintiff by saying, "As Mr. Garland has the reputation of being an honorable, kind hearted man I suppose he treats his slave kindly. I know of nothing to the contrary."[31]

McCullough denied owning any slaves, while acknowledging that in his capacity as marshal he had sold some slaves and was in fact present when Garland bought Glover. He added that, although he was familiar with the selling portion of slave trade, he had never seen a mother sold separately from her children, nor witnessed any of the other practices referred to in the questions.[32]

In the first four months of 1855, Booth would face two trials in Wisconsin. The first, a criminal one, would determine whether he had violated the Fugitive Slave Law and, if found guilty, whether he would be imprisoned, fined, or both. The civil suit would decide whether Booth owed Garland any monetary damages for his losses because he no longer had the use of Glover's services.

The civil suit depositions were received by the court two days into Booth's criminal trial, which had begun on January 9, 1855, four days after the second indictment was handed down. Because the same judge was to preside at the civil trial, a continuance was granted until April 18 while the criminal trial went forward. On Saturday, January 13, at about nine o'clock in the evening, after seven hours of deliberation, the jury brought in a verdict finding Sherman M. Booth guilty of aiding, abetting, and assisting the escape of Joshua Glover. He was sentenced to one month in jail and a fine of one thousand dollars.[33]

The civil trial eventually began in late June and lasted four days. After two days of deliberation, the jury reported that they had not agreed and were not likely to. The jury was discharged, and preparations began for a new trial. On the day following the seventy-ninth annual celebration of Independence Day, the defense challenged the new jury array and was overruled. The defense then mustered enough individual challenges to exhaust the panel after only eight jurors had been seated. The court then ordered a special panel to be issued, to be served by one Leander Le Clerc, who was described by Judge Miller as "a disinterested deputy of the Marshal." From this special venire, four additional jurors were chosen, and the trial began the following day. It was concluded on July 7 with the verdict that Booth was liable in the amount of $1,000 and costs of $246. The defense promptly filed a motion for a new trial, which was denied on August 6, and the verdict was affirmed.[34]

It took Garland another year and a half to get his judgment executed. In February of 1857, the U.S. marshal directed that Booth's presses be sold to satisfy the judgment. Ironically, it was Booth's own paper that reported that story, possibly among the last reportage to appear in the *Milwaukee Free Democrat* under his ownership.[35]

A review of newspaper accounts and available court records for the period March 1854 through early August 1855 provides much evidence that, from the outset, the verdicts finally reached in both the criminal and civil trials were predetermined. Almost 150 years ago, verbatim transcripts were not always required; as a result, sensational cases such as this were frequently extensively covered in the newspapers. The *Milwaukee Free Democrat* and *Racine Advocate*, each owned by pivotal figures in the case, devoted significant space to witnesses for each side, as well as to practically every utterance of Judge Miller. Additionally, the *Milwaukee Sentinel* was exhaustive in its coverage.

As a result of the extensive coverage available to anyone who had a few coppers for a newspaper, many citizens were conversant with every detail of the case from the first hearing in early March of 1854 through the criminal trial of January 1855 to the civil verdict in August of that year. Very few people were neutral on the topic of slavery, and those who had opinions were often extreme in their viewpoints and vociferous in the expression of them. Under such circumstances, it is easy to believe that it would have been difficult for Booth to receive an unbiased trial, as one would be defined today. This is exactly what Booth and his attorneys thought as well.

Immediately following the outcome in the criminal case, Booth's attorneys set about challenging the verdict on the basis of a number of the jurors being prejudiced against Booth long before the indictment and the trial. Five citizens, including Booth, gave affidavits regarding the biases of three grand jurors. Another eight citizens, including John Rycraft, gave affidavits concerning the prejudices of two trial jurors. One of these jurors, Joseph Treat, was the subject of seven of the affidavits. Booth also swore an affidavit that U.S. Marshal Stephen V. R. Abelman had hand selected some jurors. Deputy Marshal C. C. Cotton, in his affidavit, swore that he had not hand picked any jurors but that he was following the orders of Marshal Abelman to individually select Joseph Treat.

The seven deponents spoke of Treat in as many conversations, at six different locations, in which he talked in the strongest words about Booth's guilt, with four of them remembering Treat saying of Booth, "Damn him, he ought to go to Waupun [the state penitentiary]." Treat was also alleged by Rycraft to have said, "He wished he could get on the jury to convict him" and, "He wished he had Booth in a nine pound cannon and he would shoot him to hell, damn him."[36]

Treat, in his affidavit, declared before B. K. Miller, clerk of the district court, who was also the son of Judge Miller, that he either never remembered or never said any of the things imputed to him. He additionally denied that he had ever said he was unfit for jury duty because he had already made up his mind.[37]

Whatever else might be true of Treat, he spent a lot of his time within the judicial system. Between January 1852, two years before Glover's rescue, and November 1860, a few months before Booth was released from jail, Joseph Treat was sued at least four times. Two of these were in federal court and two in state court. Three of the suits resulted in judgments against Treat for more than twelve hundred dollars and costs. In the fourth case, the district attorney filed suit against Treat and another man for five thousand dollars in the matter of an ex-city comptroller who had apparently jumped bail and for whom they had given surety.[38]

These misfortunes not withstanding, Treat was apparently regarded by the local judiciary as an exemplar of the establishment. Not only was he individually selected as a juror by U.S. Marshal Abelman in the Glover case, but in 1857, Arthur McArthur, judge of the circuit court, appointed him as foreman of a grand jury.[39]

Our mythology of the "Wild West" contains many adages about swift retribution under color of law, one of the most famous being, "Let's give him a fair trial and then hang him." This kind of justice is generally associated with locations such as Dodge City, Kansas, Tombstone, Arizona, or any southwestern town with unpaved streets and a cemetery called Boot Hill. This, however, was Milwaukee thirty years earlier and well on its way to becoming a major port city on the Great Lakes. It had a public school system, theaters with cultural and entertainment programs, and a federal district court as well as a fully functioning state court system. However, it was still on the frontier. Fewer than ten years earlier it had graduated from the status of a territory to that of a state.

One might well ask how such an apparently civilized system could permit the travesties of justice that appear to have occurred in the federal trials of Booth and Rycraft. The answer, although not a simple one, can be found in the differing interpretations of the slavery issue and the Fugitive Slave Law as they were seen by the state and federal judicial systems. In every instance in which Glover's case came before a state court, those representing Garland's point of view lost, and those favoring Booth's interpretation won. Exactly the reverse occurred at the federal level. The Fugitive Slave Law was the law of the land. To allow it to be flouted would, in the opinion of many, have threatened the delicate balance that existed between the slaveholding states of the South and the free states of the North.

That Glover had escaped from a state that was formed on the basis of congressional compromise between the proponents of two very different systems was of crucial importance because of the ongoing debate over the status of slavery in the proposed new territories of Kansas and Nebraska and whether that status would be determined by popular sovereignty. The 1854 passage of the Kansas-Nebraska Act, by removing the provision in the Missouri Compromise that slavery would be prohibited west of Missouri, and by leaving its outcome in the hands of the voters, effectively removed congressional control of slavery in the territories and brought war that much closer.

There was also enormous pressure from the government in Washington in general and from Chief Justice Taney in particular to yield no quarter in the enforcement of the Fugitive Slave Law. The threads that held the Union together were unraveling at increasing speed. All these factors combined to make proponents on each side seek to have their viewpoint triumph while making no concessions to the other side. This unyielding attitude once again demonstrated that this was a situation in which no compromise was possible. Only one side could prevail.

As Booth and his attorneys tried to defeat slavery through the judicial system, political challenges to that institution were also being mounted with increasing vigor against the executive and legislative branches of government. The chief form of this opposition was in the newly emerging Republican Party, which was officially inaugurated under that name a few months after the capture and rescue of Joshua Glover. Glover was by no means the sole, or even primary, reason for the establishment of the party. There is, however, no doubt that the events centering around and subsequent to his capture were powerful catalysts to its creation.

The Republican Party was created from two groups that had broken away from the proslavery policies of the major parties, notably the Democrats. The first of these was the Liberty Party, founded in upstate New York about 1839. Its platform promoted an end to interstate slave trade, to the Fugitive Slave Act of 1793, and to slavery in the District of Columbia. It did not make distinctions among the rights of working-class people based on skin color. It also did not advocate colonization for black people. Gerrit Smith of New York, a prominent member who ran as the party's nominee for president in 1848, defined the party this way: "The Liberty Party actually takes the ground of the political and social equality of all men. He is not a Liberty Party man who makes political right turn on physical peculiarities; and he is not a Liberty Party man, who does not as warmly welcome a colored man as a white man to his table."[40] Sherman Booth was a member of the Liberty Party, as were a number of the men who hid Glover during his journey through southeastern Wisconsin.

The second splinter group was known as the Free-Soil Party. While they described themselves as being opposed to slavery, their opposition was qualified by concerns that today would be called racist and were, in fact, called that by members of the Liberty Party. The Free-Soil Party was founded in 1848, and its philosophy was articulated by Henry Clay and David Wilmot, who authored the proviso that bore the latter's name. This proviso was created in 1846 following the end of the Mexican War and was designed to oppose the spread of slavery to free states or territories now in existence or likely to be created. This position was adopted more because of a belief that the spread of slavery would jeopardize jobs for members of the white working class than because of any conviction that slavery was inherently wrong. Free-Soilers were much more likely to believe in colonization and in general to regard blacks as inferiors. This difference between advocates of "political anti-slavery" and abolitionism was not lost on black leaders who overwhelmingly supported the Liberty Party over the Free-Soilers.[41]

When the editor and essayist Charles Dudley Warner coined, in 1870, the now proverbial phrase "Politics makes strange bedfellows," he could have had in mind what happened next between the competing philosophies of the two groups. Recognizing that neither alone had the political muscle to survive and prosper against the Democrats, leaders of the two parties considered the previously unthinkable: a merger into a single party. This is the situation that existed in Wisconsin and elsewhere in 1854, when Joshua Glover inadvertently burst upon the scene.

In early 1854, abolitionists were already thoroughly fired up by the imminent passage of the Kansas-Nebraska bill, which would open the territories to popular sovereignty slavery. The arrest of Glover added fuel to the flames. A little more than a month after his capture and rescue, a meeting was held at Young's Hall in Milwaukee to discuss the formation of a new political party.[42] Many in attendance were members of the Liberty Party. On March 20, a little more than a week after Glover's rescue, a meeting was held in Ripon, Wisconsin, where the first Republican Party in the state was founded.[43]

By July of 1855, a state Republican convention was held in Madison and was able to field a full slate of candidates at the state level. Following that meeting, the extent of opposition to the new party and its antislavery policies became evident. The *Madison State Journal* reprinted an item from the *Waukesha Democrat* under the headline "A Meeting of the Fag-Ends" that said:

> The wise heads in examining the condition of things came to the solemn conclusion that, in this State, if all the Whigs, Free Soilers, Abolitionists, Native Americans, Calathumpians, Know Nothings, Maine Law men, fanatic, bogus democrats, and d—n fools could be united, there would be enough of them to beat the democratic party. They accordingly met at Madison on the 13th inst. And resolved that there was no Free Soil nor Whig parties, that henceforth the political parties should be Democratic and *Republican*. The name is good, but can't save them. A nigger is a nigger if you put him in a flour barrel."[44]

Although the performance of the Republican Party was less than outstanding in the November election, by early 1860 a Milwaukee paper wrote that the composition of the Republicans in the state assembly was broadly representative of many occupations including bricklayers and housejoiners. The paper also stated that the Republicans had twenty-five members who were foreign born and more than half who had been born in New York and New England, ample testimony to the broad base of the new party.[45]

By 1856 the party was able to nominate a candidate for president. Although John Fremont lost to James Buchanan nationally, in Wisconsin, the Republican ticket carried by a majority of more than thirteen thousand, and the state delegation in the House of Representatives was solidly Republican. By 1858 it was the majority party in the House. One Republican who failed that year was Abraham Lincoln, whose effort through the famous Lincoln-Douglas debates to make the Republicans the majority party in

Illinois was defeated, leading to the state legislature electing a Democrat, Stephen Douglas, as U.S. senator. Two years later, in a four-way race, Lincoln was the first Republican Party candidate elected president. This victory was followed by the secession of the Southern slaveholding states and then the Civil War.

While the party in which he had been so involved was joyfully celebrating its victory, Sherman Booth was still in jail. He had originally been sentenced to one month in jail and a fine of one thousand dollars plus the cost of prosecution. Unable or unwilling to pay the fine and costs, he remained in jail. He had been there for some time and had already served more than his sentence when friends, including several federal officials, prevailed on Booth to petition President James Buchanan for a pardon.

Booth wrote a letter to the president, asking for the pardon. Rather than restricting his plea to asking that he be released from prison, he used the occasion to defend himself in strong language, calling his conviction and sentence "unjust and illegal" and his imprisonment "an outrage on my rights, and the rights of a sovereign State." Attorney General Jeremiah S. Black replied to the local U.S. attorney, telling him that as long as Booth retained what Black regarded as his arrogance and did not limit himself to a declaration of poverty, he would not be considered for a pardon. Booth remained in prison for an additional year.[46]

On March 2, 1861, on the eve of Abraham Lincoln's inauguration and a week less than seven years after Glover's capture and rescue, outgoing president James Buchanan granted a remission of the fine and costs and freed Booth from jail.[47]

During the almost seven years these momentous events had been transpiring, Joshua Glover had been living in Canada. Although he was probably unaware of the role he had played in the build-up to the nation's Civil War, he almost certainly knew that war was raging several hundred miles south of his present home. He was also leading a busy life in the land of his newfound freedom.

9

The Promised Land

From the days of the deluge, through the years of wandering in the desert, to the length of the agony in the garden of Gethsemane, both the Old and New Testaments repeat the number forty to emphasize the duration of momentous events that shaped the history of an early people who were themselves once enslaved. Considering the presence of religion in the life of Joshua Glover, as evidenced by his church membership and various prayerful utterances, it seems appropriate that the final stage of his journey to freedom should span the dates from his March 10, 1854, capture by Garland to the April 19 evidence of his arrival in Etobicoke, Canada, a village a short distance from Toronto. It was a period of forty days encompassing a personal odyssey to yet another promised land.

When Glover did make landfall in Canada, knowledge of his existence had preceded his arrival. At least three newspapers, including those in Owen Sound, Simcoe County, and Barrie, carried condensed accounts of his capture and rescue about two weeks following those events. Additionally, the widely influential abolitionist paper *Provincial Freeman* contained an extensive account.[1] Such coverage certainly indicates a more than casual interest in the traffic on the UGRR. It also suggests the presence of a greater number of channels of potential communication between the fugitives and their benefactors than has been generally acknowledged.

While Glover was not greeted at the dock by brass bands and dignitaries, it would have been relatively easy for local people to make the connection that this travel-worn colored man, debarking from a ship flying the American flag, might be the same one who had been featured in the newspapers a week or so earlier. Such recognition would also have made it easier for him to obtain information from a sympathetic source about possible places of employment in Ontario.

Evidence of his arrival at his final destination is found in an account book of Thomas Montgomery of Etobicoke, owner of Montgomery's Inn and one of the large landholders in the area. On that date in one of his account books is found the entry, "Joshua Glover the Negro to cash 15/-."[2] The reference is to fifteen shillings, then about three dollars, and appears to be an advance against wages.[3] Typical wages in 1854 were, of course, considerably less than those of today.[4]

From this point on, much of what is known about Joshua Glover comes from the diaries, daybooks, and account books of the Montgomery family, two generations of whom were, in turn, his employers, benefactors, and caretakers throughout the next thirty-four years of his life.

Born in County Fermanagh, Ireland, in 1790, Thomas Montgomery was about twenty-two when he arrived in Quebec in 1812. From there, he walked to Chatham, a distance of some six hundred miles, carrying all his possessions on his person.[5] By the time Joshua Glover first met him in Etobicoke more than forty years after that trek, Thomas was sixty-four and a well-established businessman. He owned an inn, farmed several hundred acres, and also owned considerable real estate in the surrounding area, including Toronto. Despite Montgomery's affluence, it is unlikely that he ever forgot the conditions of his arrival in Canada and his remarkable overland journey. Such a memory may well have triggered his loan to an impoverished stranger who arrived in Etobicoke after a perilous trip.

Thomas Montgomery was one of seven brothers who settled in North America, with at least three moving to the United States. Following his marriage to Margaret Dawson, they also had seven children, four of whom died before they were a year old, with only one, William, surviving into old age. After working as a surveyor in Peel County for a number of years, Thomas moved to Etobicoke soon after the 1830 birth of William.[6] Early in the 1830s he built a large stone inn on the hill east of Mimico Creek. This was one of the first stone buildings in the area, previous constructions having been mostly log and frame. His business prospered so rapidly that by 1838 he added two wings, which included a kitchen.[7]

We have no direct knowledge why Montgomery chose Etobicoke, and particularly the village of Islington, originally called Mimico, for his three hundred-acre farm and his inn. We do, however, have the words of various writers about the area that describe both the aesthetic and practical aspects of such a setting. Responding to the question, "Where would you choose to live?" one local writer, referring to Islington, answered: "Right here before the coming of the white man. How I would have loved to have seen that virgin forest covering most of this area and Mimico creek winding through the valley furnishing the people with pure water and fish."[8] She went on to describe how the coming of the settlers resulted in destruction of the forest and inadvertent killing of the fish, following the installation of a sawmill on the creek. The area was also bounded by the Humber River and Lake Ontario, which still allowed for fishing, as well as picnicking during the warmer part of the year.

On October 17, 1847, when Bishop Strachan officially opened St. George's-on-the-Hill Anglican Church, he described it as "of rough cast construction, with the old-fashioned large windows to emit lots of light, but the most striking feature is the lofty spire rising up above the trees, in height of a hundred feet, whose tinned sides sparkled and gleamed in the sunlight so as to be visible for miles around."[9]

Noted more for his business sense than for his appreciation of aesthetic beauty, Montgomery probably made his choice based primarily on location. The inn's strategic site on the Dundas Highway, which farmers used traveling to the area mills, was an important factor in early success. Because the mills were about a mile south of Dundas, farmers were frustrated crossing the rough land to their destination, so Montgomery cut a road, called Montgomery Street and later Montgomery Lane, through his farm to make it easier for farmers to get to the mills and, not incidentally, his inn. By 1846 there were two sawmills, a blacksmith, and two shoemakers, as well as wagon makers and various tradesmen. The village population was estimated at 150.[10] As farm-to-mill traffic grew, so did the

Montgomery's Inn, the inn and tavern owned by Glover's employer and benefactor.

roads. An extension of Burnamthorpe Road first became known as New Road, and then it was called "Darky Street" after two fugitive slaves, who had found refuge in Canada, settled there. Still later it became Bigham Avenue, and only after an itinerant photographer, confused about how to title it on a postcard, called it "Picturesque Drive" was it finally permanently changed to Burnamthorpe.[11] Glover, having previously lived in the larger city of Racine, would have had no trouble fitting into this small agricultural community.

Joshua Glover was not the first American black person, nor the first fugitive slave, to make Etobicoke his home. In various censuses, quite a few listed the United States as their birthplace. The earliest of these found by a local researcher was Obadiah Henderson, born in the United States about 1783. Beginning in 1831, Henderson was able to buy twenty-five acres of farmland, subscribe to the York County Directory, marry, produce four acres of wheat and other crops in 1851, and, by 1856, retire and sell his improved land for about sixteen hundred dollars.[12]

A number of immigrants rented land from Thomas Montgomery, boarded at his inn, and drank at his tavern. The 1851 census for Etobicoke listed thirty-nine black residents in the general

Montgomery's Inn

Thomas Montgomery's son William (in beard), with his children, grandchildren, and wife.

population of twenty-five hundred.[13] This was more than triple the number recorded in 1842 and may also be evidence of an increase in the number of runaway slaves.[14]

John Dunkins (or Duncan), a black carpenter who lived in Islington, was born in the United States about 1809. He first appears in Thomas Montgomery's accounts in 1837 as an occasional tavern customer and also doing carpentry work. For five months in 1841, he kept his "Cow in pasture at 5/0 per Month 25/0."[15]

John Winston Skanks, another black carpenter, along with Dunkins built fences, gates, and a porch for Montgomery in 1838.[16] It was this penchant for making multiple entries about those who worked for him that has also preserved knowledge of Joshua Glover, which very likely would never have existed had Glover settled in a large city such as nearby Toronto.

Another source of income for Montgomery was the various forms of alcohol sold at his tavern. When these sales were on credit, he had an often colorful way of identifying the debtors by occupation or physical characteristics. His daybook for July 28, 1837, lists among others, "Smith Wooden Leg to Glas and Hay 1/0." In another entry he calls him, "James Smith a man with one leg teemster."[17]

Some of Thomas Montgomery's other identifiers include interesting descriptions and spelling variations: "Robinson a pedlar," "George the Indian," "Mr. Vanorman bedstead maker," and "Wm. Orton the man that got hurt in falling into the sellar."[18] As he came to know people better, he tended to drop these descriptions. This is certainly the case with Dunkins and Skanks, neither of whom are referred to by color. Eventually Joshua Glover is referred to by his name alone, although Thomas Montgomery's son, William, later revived his father's earlier custom when he became Glover's employer.

When Thomas described his alcohol purchases and sales at the inn, which appeared to be a significant part of his business, his switching between the new decimal system and the older English system of pounds, shillings, and pence made for some confusion, as illustrated in these entries for three different years: "18 June 1838 Received of Mr. Thomas Davis 8 barrels of beer paid him in cash for the old account which is three barrells $10 [2.10.0]"; "2 March 1839 Rec'd of John Hamilton 3 barrels whiskey 2-41 1/4 each marked 1–32 which in all would make 114 1/2 qt 2/- per gallon which is l l/8/0—apply on a note of hand I hold against him"; "21 October 1844 Castle Frank Brewery 1 barrel 25 gallons ale for 1/5 [per gallon] returned one cask."[19] As large as the inflow was, so also was the outflow.

Life in rural Canada was hard, marked by long hours of difficult physical labor and little recreation, although those with the means to do so could visit the growing city of Toronto on a day trip. One of the more frequent leisure-time activities was drinking, and Thomas Montgomery was there to fill that need. His record books give ample evidence of the drinking patterns of the local populace, both neighbors and employees. On August 10 of an unspecified year, George Silverthorne, a member of a local family, purchased a total of forty-eight glasses of potables, including beer, whiskey, brandy, wine, and peppermint for slightly over four dollars.[20] Peppermint, by the way, was not the innocent concoction its name might suggest. Thomas's recipe was: "Take about ten or eleven gallons of whiskey to about an ounce of the oil of peppermint and about 10 lb. shugger melt the shugger down. Muscavado is the best, then you may put the same quantity of water and whiskey And if too strong you can easily bring it down to the right strength."[21] The concoction sounds something like our present peppermint schnapps, without the quality control, but probably as sneaky in its effects.

Skanks, the carpenter, apparently contributed a good bit of his income to Montgomery. On July 28, 1837, he was one of six customers charging their drinks at the tavern, and he had seven glasses of beer.[22] His drinking apparently did not decrease over time, because on January 5, 1845, the following notation occurs in Montgomery's books: 'Wm. Skanks to [15] glasses of whiskey 2/6, Brandy [44] 2/0, Broke 2 Chares 5/0."[23] One can only wonder whether, because he was a carpenter, he later paid the damages from his exuberant celebration or simply fixed the chairs himself when he sobered up.

Men were not the only tipplers. On November 14, 1837, Mrs. Price charged "3 1/2 pt whis 3 1/2 pints sider," and on February 12, 1838, there was a billing for "Mrs. Grahme to 4 glasses whis," and a charge to "A Mrs. Campbell 4 Glas Beer and Lodgins."[24] In addition to the drinks he supplied, Montgomery also made food available for tavern patrons as well as lodgers, although it was hardly elegant and no bill of fare was available. His food purchases included such items as herring, pickles, and other farm and dairy products.[25] There was also the occasional wedding reception that, with its larger number of guests, produced substantial income.

In addition to being a neighborhood tavern, Montgomery's Inn was also a community center where various groups met. Chief among these was the Orange Lodge, of which Montgomery, having been born in Northern Ireland, was a member. These combined political and social meetings, which took place at regular intervals between 1836 and 1842, produced gross receipts for dinner and drinks between four and six dollars at each meeting.[26]

As with many secret and quasi-secret societies of the present day, the Orange Lodge had rules, regulations, and rituals and attendant fines and penalties for breaking them. At the Battle of the Boyne in Ireland on July 12, 1690, William III defeated the Catholic king, James II, who fled to France. This victory is celebrated annually by Orangemen as having secured Protestantism as the state religion of Great Britain. Such a celebration was held annually at Montgomery's Inn, and at one of those, the following resolution was passed: "Carried by a majority of the Lodge that any member of the said Lodge who Does get drunk on the 13th of July shall be expelled." While fighting was not expressly prohibited at less solemn times, the consequences of such behavior are dealt with severely as in the following example: "Any Orange-man Chalanging [*sic*] or Striking another Orange man who is a regular member of his Lodge is to be fined 4/11 1/2d. for the first time and for the 2d offence to be suspended for 3 months and for the 3d offence to be Expelled for Life."[27]

Thomas Montgomery was a man of enormous energy. Not only did he run a tavern where, it would seem from the book entries, he was frequently in attendance, but he was also a purveyor of food and livestock to many in the community, including his tenant farmers. He also farmed between two hundred and three hundred acres and owned his own threshing machine as early as 1840.[28] He functioned as a money lender to his employees as well, deducting the debt from their wages, along with their rent and board.[29] In spite of the numerous records that survive, there are many gaps in the continuity of entries, both for entire years and within years.

The inn on Dundas Street was not Thomas Montgomery's only commercial enterprise. There is evidence of five other business properties: three taverns, a sawmill, and a store. The taverns were located in Brampton, Churchville, and Toronto. Two of these, the Brampton House and the Canada House in Toronto, were also hotels.[30] Montgomery did not operate these himself but leased them to others, in one instance furnishing the Brampton House with pieces from Montgomery's Inn, which ceased operation as a hotel before he acquired Brampton House.[31]

In 1870, Montgomery received an anonymous letter in reference to Brampton House saying: "Your house is now a whore house and a nuisance to the village. get these people out of it who are now in it and get some decent people to take it over at a nominal amt and it will profit you in the end."[32]

This is not the only difficulty Montgomery had in the management of his properties. Throughout his career as a businessman, from its inception in the early 1830s until his death at age eighty-six, Montgomery was intermittently embroiled in difficulties—commercial and financial, civil and criminal. One fact that emerges from Montgomery's business records is that he was an indifferent record keeper of his large holdings. Something is known of the extent of his real estate dealings from the fact that between May 8, 1854, and September 25, 1856, he repaid to the Permanent Building Society loans totaling more than thirty-five thousand dollars in five payments, a very large sum at that time.[33]

In civil actions he was both plaintiff and defendant. When money was owed to him, he was vigorous in pursuit of its recovery, a trait he had in common with Glover's former owner. One debtor, Archibald Campbell, was committed to the Provincial Lunatic Asylum. Montgomery, determined to collect his money, tried to get into the institution to serve a legal document. He was prevented from getting near Campbell, the medical superintendent stating Campbell was in possession of a certificate of lunacy and being served with a legal document would have a negative effect on his mind.[34]

When money was owed by Montgomery to others, his response was at times not quite so swift. This was also true occasionally in protecting his own interests. In 1862 Montgomery was informed that proceedings were about to be started against him for unlawfully detaining a trunk, and in 1876, according to a note: "I can only remind you that June is coming very fast and the first of July will soon be here. If you lose all your claims dont blame me."[35]

A vigorous opponent not only when civilly wronged, Thomas Montgomery could be quite vengeful when crossed. He is known to have made threats to burn down a place he owned if the tenant did not vacate it. He was suspected of two arson attempts and charged with one of them. Two notes, determined by the court to be in Montgomery's handwriting, survive. In the first, he says: "If this tenant is not stopped it shall be by Fire we give two weeks notice 4th May 1839."[36] Another reads: "To Truman Wilcox Sir we pity you if you dont stop this Tenant, if it is not stopped it shall be shortly burnt." He was tried October 22, 1839, before the court of Oyer and Terminer on a felony charge of arson. The jury reached a verdict of not guilty, even though the accelerant was of a type used only by Thomas Montgomery.[37]

Researchers who have studied Montgomery as an example of a nineteenth-century entrepreneur have concluded that he was "a rough and selfish businessman unafraid to pursue his interests at other peoples' expense."[38] In spite of this judgment, he was not without friends and enjoyed a moderately successful social life. He bequeathed a substantial estate to William, and judging from records that will be detailed later, he was, for the times, a relatively fair and just employer of Joshua Glover. He showed no evidence of discriminating against him on the basis of race, behavior not always characteristic of other residents of the area during the time that the Fugitive Slave Law was causing large numbers of slaves to seek safety in Canada.

When Glover rented his home from Montgomery, he found himself in surroundings that were not unfamiliar to him. For about two dollars a month, he rented a one-story house complete with cookstove. He was located within sight of the Humber River, as he had been close to the Root River in Racine. He was also not far from a sawmill. He had black neighbors, whom he could invite to his home to play cards, but in this instance he need not fear the police and his erstwhile master descending upon him in the middle of the night.

Since 1820 slavery had been virtually eliminated throughout the provinces of Upper and Lower Canada, as British North America was known at that time.[39] An act of the imperial parliament abolished all slavery in 1833. That same year, Upper Canada, where Glover would eventually live, passed an act to provide for the capture and extradition of "Fugitive Offenders from Foreign Countries." This was in part a concession to the United States designed to improve relations between the two countries that now had different views and laws regarding slavery. Because Canada did not wish to be seen as toadying to their neighbor to the south, a clause was included that left judgment on the merits of each case to the governor, who was free not to return a slave if he "deemed it inexpedient to do so."[40] While this act was, in theory, designed for all offenders, it was created particularly to deal with fugitive slaves. In most instances a governor acted with compassion toward those whose only crime had been to steal themselves, something that was not a crime under Canadian law.

Robbery and horse stealing, if engaged in as a necessary adjunct to escape, were also not generally regarded as crimes worthy of extradition. One slave was returned in 1842 because he had also stolen a watch and an extra saddle, regarded by Canadian authorities as not necessary to his escape.[41]

By 1849 the government had enacted a stronger extradition law, but no fugitive slave was ever surrendered to the United States under this law.[42] Following the passage of the U.S. Fugitive Slave Act in 1850, which gave slave owners the power to enlist the federal government in their efforts to reclaim their property from any state, Canada became an even more frequent destination on the UGRR.

From 1850 through 1853 a small number of fugitive slaves were returned to the states improperly. In each instance, the Canadian officials responsible for the action were either removed from their jobs or tried for assault. In the most important case of all, a fugitive slave accused of murder in the states was found not extraditable, even though this decision came dangerously close to breaching a treaty between the two nations.[43] Effectively, this outcome produced the result that any crime committed by a fugitive slave to effect his escape was not an extraditable offense. It was for this reason that Glover, when he arrived in 1854, could go to bed at night secure in the knowledge that he would not awaken to a blow on the head and manacles on his limbs. Secure though he may have been in his freedom, he did not have equal assurance that he would lead his life free of prejudice, discrimination, and racism.

When blacks first began to arrive in Canada in 1783, they came not as fugitives running in panic from their masters but as patriots rewarded by the British for their services to the Crown during the Revolutionary War. Sir Guy Carleton, commander-in-chief of the British forces in North America, guaranteed that all slaves seeking protection would be given freedom. Before the promise was put into action, however, General George Washington met with Carleton to discuss with particular reference to Negro slaves how withdrawal of British forces could be accomplished without "carrying away any Negroes or other property of the American Inhabitants."[44] Washington failed in his effort to get the British to renege on their promise to the slaves, and some 3,500 were given their freedom by the British and settled in Nova Scotia and New Brunswick.

A similar event took place during the War of 1812, when the commander of the British fleet made an offer to slaves similar to the offer made by Sir Guy Carleton more than twenty years earlier. This was also protested by the Americans, who resorted to international arbitration. This resulted in the emperor of Russia finding that the British owed the United States more than one million dollars for the more than three thousand slaves who took Britain up on its offer.[45]

While loyalists from the Revolution and refugees from the War of 1812 were settling in the eastern part of Canada, the trickle of fugitive slaves that had been making its way into Ontario since 1790 began to grow after the Missouri Compromise of 1820. It increased more rapidly after the passage of the Fugitive Slave Act in 1850. Although welcomed at first to a land that had abolished slavery many years before, the increasing number of blacks working for lower wages than the white population gradually produced an increase in stereotypes, prejudice, and discrimination.

In 1849 the sheriff of Chatham called a meeting to prevent Negroes from owning land.[46] When black children were enrolled in schools, a number of white parents removed their children. By 1850, the Ontario Common School Act permitted separate schools for blacks, and if no school was available, then blacks were educated at different times or sat on segregated benches.[47]

The "promised land" that was to be found by following the North Star turned out not to be quite as promised. There was, however, one thing that was true. The fugitives were slaves no more. They were free, able to work for a living, to pull up stakes when they wished. They were still subject to some of the constraints existing in the States, both northern and southern, but nonetheless free men, women, and children.

This difference was perhaps best expressed by John H. Hill, a skilled carpenter, when he wrote to William Still saying, "I wants [*sic*] you to let the whole United States know we are satisfied here because I have seen more Pleasure since I came here than I saw in the U. S. the 24 years that I served my master." In a later letter he added, "It is true that I have to work very hard for comfort but I would not exchange with ten thousand slaves that are equel [*sic*] with their masters. I am Happy, Happy."[48]

Pockets of prejudice notwithstanding, the overwhelming sentiment of the former fugitives was best expressed in 1851 at the first North American Convention of Colored Freemen, held at Lawrence Hall in Toronto. In addition to those already living in Canada, there were attendees from the Northern states and England. Not only did the members declare that Canada was the best place in the world for blacks to live, the convention leaders also stated "that the British government was the most favorable in the civilized world to the people of colour and was thereby entitled to the entire confidence of the Convention."[49]

10

Sweet and Bitter: Life on the Farm

It is most unlikely that Joshua Glover simply wandered by accident onto the property of Thomas Montgomery. From the time he left the ship until he reached Montgomery's farm, it is likely that he received information about a place where work was often available, where both blacks and whites were employed, and where workers were treated equitably. In fact, Thomas Montgomery had at one time owned property in Collingwood and may have been known there. There were also a number of former fugitive slaves living there. If Glover debarked there for the sixty-mile overland journey to Etobicoke, one or more residents could easily have told him about Montgomery.

By the time Glover arrived in Etobicoke, a small town with several villages, about nine miles west of Toronto, there were already three dozen blacks from the States living there. Some, like the carpenters John Dunkins and Winston Skanks, had been there for fifteen years or more, were married, had children, and owned property.[1] Others rented houses with an acre or more of land, which they farmed. Dunkins eventually rented twenty acres of land, which he worked in addition to his carpentry business. He was listed as a farmer in the Tax Assessments of 1861 and produced six acres of spring wheat, along with fifty bushels of carrots in addition to other vegetables.[2]

Seeing the abundant crops that could be grown in this harsh but fertile land, it would not have taken the former foreman of a three hundred-acre farm in Missouri very long to figure out that he had found a place where he could put his talents to good use on his own behalf. He began by renting a house in the village of Lambton Mills from Thomas Montgomery for about two dollars a month. It was a simple, one-story structure, similar to those that Montgomery rented to other tenants. It had a wood-burning cookstove that also served as a source of heat in winter. The first dwelling that he rented was situated on an acre and a half of land. In addition to the crops he planted, he also worked for wages as a farm laborer on Thomas Montgomery's extensive property.

The first surviving records of Glover's work for Montgomery show that on August 17, 1856, he "cut ten acres of pease [*sic*] at $2.00/acre and nine and three-quarters acres of grass at $1.50/acre." On September 3 he cut oats for twenty-two dollars. After Montgomery had deducted various cash advances to Glover through September 20, he had five dollars cash coming to him.[3] While that might not seem like a lot of money today, with mid-nineteenth-century wages for an adult male laborer running between fifty cents and seventy-five cents a day, such an accounting meant that he had fed, sheltered, and clothed himself for a month and still had almost two weeks' wages in his possession. Of course, although sheltered, he may not have been current on his rent. The Montgomerys, both father and son, were not regular collectors of rent, sometimes going many months before settling the rent account. In one instance in 1857, Glover paid up his rent in April and not again until the end of December.[4]

Joshua Glover was possessed of energy, stamina, and strength that would be a source of wonder even in this era of long-lived, healthy people. In one week of October 1856, when he was in his early forties, he worked "in front of the house," "2 days in the bush," "2 days thrashing [threshing]," and "cut 52.5 cords of wood @$.60/cord."[5] A work week then was figured at six days, and days may have lasted as long as the sun shone. Following work, he went home and cooked his dinner. Judging from his purchases from Thomas, Glover ate a lot of bacon, made his own bread or biscuits, and once in a while had pork chops. Sometimes he may have shared a meal with another bachelor or been the guest of one of the married couples who had their own homes nearby. When he first began to rent, he had no crops to harvest and no pigs to slaughter and therefore bought more food from Montgomery.

In spite of the many hours that Joshua Glover worked, he did find time for recreation. Undoubtedly he drank and played cards at night with friends, but without having to lock his door against unwelcome callers. On October 1, 1858, Joshua borrowed three dollars from Thomas to attend the fair.[6] This was no run-of-the-mill county fair that he had taken an entire day off work to attend. This was the annual exhibition of the Agricultural Association of Upper Canada, which had been held in Toronto for many years and was the largest single gathering to occur in the area. In 1852, the attendance on the busiest day was estimated at thirty thousand people. Six years later, when Glover attended, the crowds were somewhat smaller because of a tremendous downpour, which reduced the attendance on the first full day.[7]

Imagine Glover's awe and pleasure at the size of the gathering. This was the first time he was in a crowd of any appreciable size when he had not been a major focus of attention, as had been true previously when he was sold to Garland on the St. Louis Courthouse steps in 1850 and when the walls of the jail came tumbling down in Milwaukee in 1854.

There was certainly no shortage of things to see and do at the fair. When Glover had been a slave on Garland's farm, there were many horses to be looked after, and he might well have been interested in the horse-judging exhibit at the fair. Having lived in the States, he might also have shared the judges' impression that the horses exhibited were of a very inferior quality and could have been improved by importing stock from the United States.[8]

There were yacht races on Lake Ontario and the judging of produce, as well as displays of the latest farm implements. One of the great wonders was the Palace of Industry, also called the Crystal Palace, which housed many of the exhibits. From ground to roof, it was fifty-five feet high and enclosed close to forty thousand square feet of space, undoubtedly the most magnificent structure Glover had ever seen. All of this he could marvel at for twenty-five cents admission. Had he waited until the second week, he could have gotten in for half that amount.[9]

Even though one tends to think of rural life in the mid-nineteenth century as being slow-moving and bucolic, there were hazards to be dealt with whenever one visited a big city and one of its popular events. Not only did several ordinary citizens have their pockets picked, in spite of prominent placards urging people to protect their valuables, but an officer of the customs house had a valuable watch lifted.[10] Some mishaps were even more serious. A teacher, returning to his home following a day at the fair, was running to catch his train. He attempted to swing up onto the engine, slipped, and fell to his death between the driving wheels and the platform.[11]

Upon his return from the fair, Glover swung right back into the routine of life on a farm, working hard for long hours, eating his simple suppers, and pursuing other interests as time permitted. An inspection of Montgomery's books for the autumn of 1859 and early 1860, however, reveals an interesting change in the amount and variety of Glover's purchases. The frequency with which he bought flour and bacon increased, and a purchase of ten pounds of beef entered his diet for the first time, followed a month later by an equal amount of mutton.[12] These changes are possible evidence of an additional person living with him.

On Christmas Eve of 1859, soul food came to Etobicoke. Joshua purchased "4 pig faces" for fifty cents.[13] What are now called pigs' heads may well have been part of a celebration meal for Christmas, shared with others, or they may have been a wedding dinner. It is not known just when Joshua married, but he is listed in the 1861 census as being married to Ann Glover, who was twenty-three years old and white and a member of Church of England.[14]

With one exception, there had been no indications, either in St. Louis or Racine, that Glover had been previously married. In December of 1854, a Racine abolitionist newspaper announced that Glover's wife and children had joined him in Canada.[15] This appears to be more of a disinformation item designed to discomfort proponents of slavery rather than an item of fact. Unlike Joshua, Ann was able to read and write.[16] She may well have been one of the many Canadian women of Irish parentage who migrated west and entered domestic service.

Marriages between former slaves and white women were not uncommon. In 1871 four families were tenants on Concession C Lot 10 of Montgomery's holdings. In each case the husband was black and the wife white and Irish. One of the men was a cooper, two were farm laborers, and one was a laborer. One of these families was Joshua and Ann Glover.[17]

It has been acknowledged that the Irish in Canada in the nineteenth century were, like blacks, victims of discrimination.[18] This is a situation that would have been readily recognized by many Irish residing in New York City in the same era.

Unfortunately, Montgomery's records are sparse for 1861–64. In 1865 they appear again but give relatively little information about the particular work Glover did, although there are two entries in the fall of 1867 indicating that Ann Glover also worked for Montgomery from time to time. She was apparently paid at a rate somewhat less than that of her husband, a not-uncommon event, even then.[19] As Glover's employment with the Montgomery family lengthened, the entries in the books became more casual. This may be in part because they tend to be repetitive, but it may also be because William had taken more responsibility for record keeping. The specific work Joshua did is not listed as often. In the beginning of 1868, there is a note: "Joshua Glover is hired at the rate of $10 pr month for the summer 6 mos. & $8.00 pr month for the winter 6 mos."[20]

Money and goods such as food, tobacco, boots, and shirting material that Glover was advanced against his labor still occurred on the debit side of the ledger, with items for Ann included as well. There were also signs that Ann may have had some skills as a seamstress; on two occasions they purchased shirting, presumably for Joshua, although Ann may have made a shirtwaist for herself as well.[21]

In 1871, the one-and-a-half-acre plot on which they lived, one acre of which was devoted to raising crops, produced sixty bushels of potatoes and fourteen bushels of turnips, carrots, and other root vegetables. They also raised pigs, slaughtering nineteen of them during the year.[22] The life of the couple appeared to run a steady course, including the typical things that a rural, working-class couple would do in the late-nineteenth century—working, eating, sleeping, possibly going to church, occasionally entertaining friends. All in all, it was an ordinary life.

Ordinary, that is, until December 6, 1872. On that day, Ann Glover, Joshua's friend, companion, and wife of more than twelve years, died. According to her physician, Dr. M. H. Aikins, the cause of death was inflammation of the lungs from exposure during an accident five days earlier. She was listed as being thirty-five at the time of her death, which would have made Joshua about fifty-eight.[23] No available newspaper carried a story of the accident-induced death of one Irish-Canadian woman married to a former fugitive slave. The actual details will not likely ever be known, other than that she was discovered and treated for the pneumonia that she contracted from the incident, until she succumbed five days later.

Within the week, Joshua borrowed a dollar from William Montgomery to purchase a grave, enabling him to bury Ann in the cemetery of St. George's Church in nearby Islington.[24] Something else happened then as well. He did not work again until December 14. He also stopped buying flour, bacon, and other staples for three months. On March 17, 1873, he bought flour, which he continued to do intermittently through 1874.[25] Part of the reason for this may have been that he was still raising produce and slaughtering his own hogs, and another reason may have been that he was no longer coupled.

Even in the absence of any written words about Ann's death from anyone present at the time, it is obvious that it was a blow from which Glover did not recover easily. He returned to work a couple of weeks after Ann's death. It was typical of him, and probably others as well, to work fewer days a month during the winter than in the planting and harvesting months. However, when spring began to arrive in 1873, his days of work in March and April dropped drastically, to fewer than in those months in the two previous years. Joshua Glover may have been ill, or he might still have been grieving. His had been a hard life, and he was not unfamiliar with tragedy and death. He had probably seen old slaves die on their blankets on the floors of their cabins, and he might have watched field hands die of exhaustion from overwork, infants and children die of malnutrition, and slaves die of punishments received for insolence or attempted escape. From what is known, however, the death of a family member was a new burden to bear.

As time passed, Glover's grief lessened, and he seemed to regain the former rhythm of his work days. In 1874 he moved to a different cabin with an acreage totaling four and a half.[26] By 1875 he was working again the same number of days monthly as he had prior to Ann's death, although the nature of the work was not specified, and all his debits were cash, with none allocated to staples or clothing.[27] The following year he whitewashed his cabin, with William charging him twenty-five cents for the brush.[28]

Now over sixty, Joshua still had amazing stamina. On November 3, 1877, he split one thousand rails at one dollar per one hundred.[29] Three weeks later, he split another five hundred.[30] During this year, William once again began listing the jobs that Glover did for him, and it began to appear that while Joshua might have been working fewer days each month than had been customary, he was continuing to do work that required both strength and endurance. He cradled wheat and barley, a method of using a scythe and a wooden frame to bundle grain; picked stones off the fields; dug out stumps; and dug a cellar under a shed. All these jobs were done between April and September.[31] Often the money he was paid for this appeared to equal the money he owed to William. It almost seems that William was finding or making work for Josh so he could repay his rent and other advances made to him. On November 8, 1877, Thomas Montgomery, his original employer, died at the age of eighty-seven and was buried by the same church as Ann Glover.[32]

Through 1878 Joshua continued to work, but for many fewer days, doing some harvesting, rail splitting, and posthole digging. In late August he spent three days assisting in the erection of a monument for Thomas at the Islington Burial Grounds.[33] Such an occasion would probably produce reflections regarding the man who had been his employer for more than twenty-three years, as well as thoughts about how differently his life had turned out after he had made the decision to steal himself from B. S. Garland.

There is one remarkable piece of evidence that indicates that some time after Ann's death Joshua had recovered sufficiently from its effects on him to enter another relationship. The Schedule of Deaths for Etobicoke for 1881 lists the death on February 6 of Mary Ann Glover from stomach ulcers after five weeks of illness. She was forty-five and was listed as having been born in Kings County, Ireland.[34]

In the space allotted for each deceased person listed on the schedule, there are also headings to list rank or profession and religious denomination. For the other decedents on the same page, these are filled out appropriately. In the entries for Mary Ann Glover, the registrar chose, in the space for surname, to also list her maiden name of Mary Ann Wattes. In the space for rank or profession, rather than leaving it blank, as had been done with others who were not employed, he entered, "Living with colored man named Joshua Glover." Instead of entering a religion for her, he penned, "Don't know. Buried in St. George's Graveyard, Etobicoke." While one could speculate endlessly regarding the registrar's motives in departing from custom, one can only be grateful that, in doing so, he provided further evidence of the resilience of Glover in the face of adversity.

As each year passed, the records covering Glover's work for William Montgomery became more sketchy, with fewer dates covered. He still worked from time to time, mostly cutting wood, clearing stumps, and cutting posts. There are no entries available after November 1882, when he worked eight days for fifty cents a day.[35] Allowing for William Montgomery being a somewhat indifferent record keeper, it is also likely that Joshua was slowing down. He was by then about sixty-eight and had employed his body to earn his keep for most of those years.

Although there is no further work record available, a small incident occurred sometime in the early to mid-1880s that illustrates one more aspect of Joshua Glover, this time as both an oral historian and a dispeller of myths about being black. The Reverend G. Moore Morgan was a small boy when his father died. He remembered his father's funeral at St. George's Church, and he remembered moving with his mother after that to the little town of Lambton Mills, where Glover also lived. One of his earliest memories was "sitting on a colored man's knee in our basement kitchen." The Reverend continued: "He had little tufts of whiskers that looked like white cotton wool stuck on his face. Mother said that I asked, 'Is your tongue black?' and that he stuck out his tongue to let me see it, and also showed me that the palms of his hands were white. He had escaped from slavery by the underground to Canada. We called him old Josh Lubber."[36]

Joshua Glover's life in Canada was much like that of any other uneducated, laboring, tax-paying citizen. It was, to other average people, not all that interesting. To Glover himself, on the other hand, what may have been the most marvelous thing about it was its lack of drama and its predictability. There was no worry about being sold away to a cotton or sugar plantation in the Lower South because he had not been enthusiastic in his response to an order. There was no threat of physical punishment. His cabin was heated in the winter and dry during the spring rains. He had ample food, a table to eat it from, and a bed to sleep in. He could indulge himself in a drink when he wished. He sometimes had money in his pocket and could choose how to spend it. Most of all, he knew that the body that laid itself to rest at night would awaken the next morning still free. He had no guarantee against personal tragedy or death, but he had freedom. For Joshua Glover, that would never be an ordinary life. He would soon have reason to cherish his freedom from enslavement even more.

11

A "Stabbing Affray"

On Saturday, May 24, 1884, there were many ways to enjoy a holiday in Toronto and its environs. One could take a boat excursion, see a play, listen to a temperance lecture, hear a military band honor Queen Victoria on her birthday, or engage in a host of other activities to one's liking. Edward Caswell and Victor Blackhall thought it would be an excellent day for a picnic.[1] Even though the forecast was for showers that day, they packed a basket and headed, along with two other friends, for a spot they knew overlooking the Humber River, near Lambton Mills.

Having finished their meal and repacked their hamper about six fifteen, the young men, Caswell, a printer, and Blackhall, a bookbinder, began to stroll along the riverbank. As they were passing near a shanty, their conversation was interrupted by the sounds of a man and woman quarreling, with the woman sometimes screaming. Entering the hovel they found John Howard, a man in his fifties lying half on a bed, a pool of blood beneath him. The source of the blood was a deep gash in his abdomen. The woman, Mary Butler, considerably younger than the victim, was intoxicated and was accusing Josh Glover of having stabbed her "husband," with whom she had been living for about a year. Howard, who was conscious, said he had been stabbed by "Old Josh." He said he was dying and begged for help in saving his life. Butler and another occupant went to summon the police, while others went for a doctor to minister to Howard. Glover, meanwhile, wandered off into the woods. By the time the constable arrived from Islington, Glover had been found lying in the woods with a double-bladed jackknife and a partially filled whiskey bottle on his person. He appeared too intoxicated to realize what had occurred, and witnesses were in agreement that all the parties appeared drunk. Neighbors later said that all three were prone to excesses in liquor.[2]

From the piecemeal stories of the three, there began to emerge a somewhat confused account of events. Mary Butler said there had been a grudge existing on Josh's part for the previous twelve months. There was some initial confusion as to whether Glover had also been stabbed. He was apparently questioned first by Charles Westwood, another picnicker whom he told that he had been stabbed. He then said no one could say "Old Josh" had ever stabbed anyone, that he had been there a number of years, never doing harm to anyone. Glover told Alfred Price, employed in his father's tailoring business and a neighbor of Caswell, that Howard had kicked him down Dundas Street eighteen years earlier. Glover denied that he had been stabbed and also at first that he had stabbed Howard. Glover turned his knife over to Price, who found no blood on it when he inspected it. Later in the interrogation, Glover admitted to the stabbing. When Constable Robert Bell arrived with a warrant for Glover's arrest, he needed the assistance of J. D. Evans, the deputy reeve of Etobicoke, in getting Glover to his feet.[3]

Howard said there had been a quarrel over a trivial matter a short time earlier, and that evening while he was standing at his door, Glover came to him, asked for the woman, and then suddenly drew a knife and stabbed him. Glover maintained that he was being restrained from leaving the house by Howard and another man because he would not pay additional money the men requested, possibly for whiskey or female companionship. It appeared at this point that further evidence would have to await trial.

Howard was placed in a village wagon for transport to the hospital. Glover, who had been handcuffed by the constable, was loaded into the same wagon for his trip to jail. At first Glover seemed confused about the situation, saying he did not care if they hung him in the morning. Afterward, he asked for a gun and said he would like to shoot himself; then, leaning over Howard as he lay in the bottom of the wagon, he said fervently, "The Lord bless you, John."[4]

The Toronto jail register for the next day has the following entry: "1884 May 25th Joshua Glover, Lambton Mills, Labourer, coloured male, age 70, b. U.S., widowed, intemperate. Never before committed."[5]

It cannot be known precisely how Glover was feeling that night, but it is known from the newspaper accounts that, in addition to being drunk, he was also depressed and distraught. The accounts reveal further that there were some remarkable parallels between events on that night and the night of his capture almost exactly thirty years earlier. In both instances he was in a shanty located near a body of water, drinking with friends, or those he believed to be so, and he was also restrained with handcuffs and was being taken to jail. Although the condition now called posttraumatic stress disorder had not been so named then, part of his reaction could well have been triggered by the similarities between the situations, in combination with his intoxication.

William Montgomery must have been a man with his fingers on the pulse of every activity in the area, for he knew of Glover's arrest on the day it happened, two days before it appeared in the newspaper. In his minute book for that date he wrote, "I heard that old Josh was taken to jail to night for assault on Jack Howard."[6] It is true that Lambton Mills and Islington were small villages in the township of Etobicoke, on the outskirts of Toronto, but for Montgomery to learn of Glover's plight before he went to bed that night, others who knew of his interest in and concern for "old Josh" must have hastened to him with the news.

If there was ever any doubt that a special relationship existed between Joshua Glover and William Montgomery, it was removed by the diary entry for Monday, May 26: "Bot 2 shirts and necktie for old Josh who is in jail. Mr. Tilt is to defend him."[7] James Tilt, Queen's Counsel, a member of the Toronto firm of Crowther, Tilt and McArthur, had been the Montgomery family's attorney and agreed to take the case.[8] At its conclusion, when Montgomery asked for a bill, Tilt declined to charge for his services.[9] This was the same barrister who had helped Thomas Montgomery out of his legal difficulties more than twenty years earlier.[10] For a former fugitive slave with few assets of his own and long before the availability of public defenders, this was a boon beyond belief.

A few days later, the preliminary investigation was held in Islington before Justice of the Peace J. D. Evans. Mary Butler testified to her version of events, exculpating herself and Howard and making no mention of another party being present. J. M. Cotton, M.D., who had attended to Howard at the scene, described the nature of the wound and his belief that it was not immediately dangerous. Blackhall recalled Glover saying that Howard had beat him when a boy. Glover, who declined to make a statement himself, was said to have told the constable he was in the house and Howard and his visitor would not let him out because he would not pay enough money. He was said to have picked up something and struck Howard with it. Glover was committed for trial and remanded to the county jail.[11] When his possessions were inventoried, besides the clothes he wore, he had on his person a pipe and seventy-five cents.[12]

On that day, William Montgomery made another entry in his minute book, which appears to indicate that he was either at that day's hearing or had spoken to someone who was, because he made a comment not reported in the newspaper. In addition to mentioning the remand to jail, he added, "It seems from what Darling says that the house that Howard kept was a nuisance."[13] This notation, taken along with comments by Glover plus the contents of the Police News column for the date of the stabbing, raises some interesting speculations as to whether all the factors responsible for what the newspaper called "a stabbing affray" were completely accounted for by the testimony of any single witness or news account. That item reported: "About 4 o'clock on Saturday morning, P. C.'s Anderson and Young raided a house of ill-fame kept in Chestnut Street, and the following parties were arrested: Lillie Butler, keeper, Lillie Butler, Jr., Jennie Shea, Ellen Reid as inmates, and Fred Maclean and Fred Harper as frequenters. They were taken to No. 2 Station."[14] A similar item in another paper noted that the same Lillie Butler of 128 Chestnut Street was a one-eyed woman with an infant in her arms.[15]

Although Mary Butler had lived with Howard for a year and called him her husband, it was generally acknowledged they were not married. Whether she was related to the Butlers of Chestnut Street is not known. One report said that when Glover came to the house, "he asked for the woman."[16] It was also reported at his initial hearing that he was not permitted to leave because he would not pay enough money. While he may have gone to Howard's to drink to the Queen's health, the fact that the house was described as "a nuisance" may also indicate he was there for an additional purpose.

Glover went to trial one month after the stabbing. Montgomery visited him at least once while he was awaiting trial, and on that occasion he wrote in his pocket diary: "Bot a pair of Drawers and gave them to Old Josh."[17] The trial was held before Chief Justice James Cameron.

Although no transcript of the trial was located, Justice Cameron did keep a bench book in which he summarized the testimony of each witness.[18] Howard said he had known Glover for more than ten years, that they lived less than a quarter mile from each other, and that Glover was at his place two to three times a week. They had fished together often and gone on drinking sprees together. He testified that he had done nothing to bring about the stabbing and that Glover did it quite suddenly. He added that Glover had never mentioned his grudge before. He was not asked, nor did he testify to, whether he had beaten Glover many years earlier, but he continued to maintain they had always been on good terms with each other. Mary Butler's testimony was quite similar to Howard's, with the addition that Glover had called her some "bad names." She also changed her testimony from her earlier deposition, in which she said she had seen the stabbing, to now claiming the stabbing had occurred while she was out of the house and that on her return, she tried to take the knife from Glover and received a scratch on her knuckle.[19]

The remaining witnesses for the Crown were the two picnickers, Caswell and Blackhall; Dr. Cotton, the physician who had attended Howard; and Constable Bell. Caswell said there had been a nephew present, who was not on the scene when he arrived, lending credence to Glover's claim of another person present. Blackhall said Glover was talking a lot of nonsense at the scene. Cotton repeated the testimony given at his deposition, including his opinion that there was nothing in the shape of the wound to indicate whether it had been caused by Glover or another. Constable Bell reported in detail his observations of Glover at the scene, including saying he had previously known Glover as "an inoffensive person."[20]

After the Crown rested, the defense presented only three witnesses. Their words, as well as their identities, were of great interest to those gathered. The first was Charles Ware (or Weir), a shopkeeper who had been a constable for fourteen years and had known Glover that long as well. Next was Matthew Canning, reeve of Etobicoke. Not only a prominent political figure, Canning was a member of the grand jury that indicted Glover.[21] Finally, as might be expected, was the man who was always present when Joshua was in need, William Montgomery. Each spoke of the length of his acquaintance with Glover, of his inoffensive manner, and of how out of character it would be for him to commit such an act.

Following the completion of testimony, the jury found Glover guilty of wounding without intent and not guilty of the serious felony charge of intent. Judge Cameron sentenced him to three months at the Central Prison.[22]

The outcome of this case was, to say the least, remarkable: A former fugitive slave, who had been living a hand-to-mouth existence for years, who had a reputation for being an excessive drinker, and who had seriously wounded a white man, received a trial within a month, was defended by a well-known counsel, had three prominent citizens appear on his behalf, including one who may have had a conflict of interest in the case, and received a verdict of guilty of a misdemeanor, followed by only a short sentence. This was more than luck. This was likely the result of a collaborative effort on the part of the establishment, probably orchestrated by William Montgomery, to do right by a man who, in spite of his low status, stood high in the affections of the community.

There was one other item of note in Judge Cameron's bench book. In the seven handwritten pages summarizing the testimony, the judge had placed an X at the margins of seven lines. Five of those marks were adjacent to comments referring to Glover's demeanor when using alcohol or his inebriated condition at the time of the crime. These marks, which could have identified responses to cross-examination, could also have been indicative of the judge's attempt to frame a rationale for his sentence based on Glover's condition at the time of the crime and the absence of a prior history of violence, even when intoxicated.

Glover had not been in prison a month when Montgomery wrote in his minute book, "I saw the Old Man Josh at the Central Prison he has been very sick."[23] Unfortunately, he wrote in his usual brief style and did not note the nature of the illness. Whatever the cause, Josh did recover and was assigned to work in the prison garden, where he served out his time. William saw Josh again in September before his discharge and later that day went to the fair.[24] Josh had physical examinations at both the beginning and end of his term. On entry he was described as being seventy-one years old, in good health, and five feet nine inches in height at 147 pounds. On discharge he weighed 152 pounds.[25]

12

The End of the Line

When Glover was released from jail toward the end of September, he likely returned to his cabin, having no other place to go. He had no money for rent or food. He was also reaching an age when it was becoming increasingly difficult for him to work. Not only age but also intermittent illness decreased his ability to support himself. He had been an able employee of the Montgomery family for more than thirty years. Over that span of time, the terms that Thomas and then William Montgomery used to refer to Glover in their diaries and ledgers form successive sketches of the evolution of their feelings about him. When Thomas first encounters him, he is "Joshua Glover, the negro." As he comes to know Josh better, he becomes "Joshua Glover the coloured man," and then simply "Joshua Glover." When William begins to make the entries, he is familiarized as "Josh"; then as age overtakes him, he becomes "Old Josh." As the end approaches and William has to look after him more, he is "poor old Josh."

Following his release from jail in the fall of 1884, until the end of 1887, when Glover was approaching eighty, there were no further ledger entries regarding Josh being paid for work done. The absence of entries notwithstanding, it is likely that William Montgomery provided Josh pocket money from time to time.

On Monday, January 30, 1888, after referring to the disposition of three bags of oats, Montgomery wrote in his daybook, "Gave Old Josh (the old coloured man) one suit of old clothes & 2 shirts and $1 in Cash."[1] On the following day, after noting that he had "paid Howland and Elliott 30 cents for chopping 3 bags of

119

oats," he penned the entry, "Old Josh the Coloured Man went to the County House."[2]

When the County House was first established in 1850, it was called the York County Industrial Home. It became known to the locals as the County Home, the Poor House, or the County Home for the Aged and was located in Newmarket, about six miles from where Glover lived.

The Industrial Home was an early experiment in social services for the poor and neglected. As such, it operated largely on the basis of the common community attitude that people were to blame for their poverty, and, while Christian principles may have dictated that they be cared for when they became a burden, they should not expect gracious treatment. In 1883, two years after the building in which Joshua would live was built, eighty people were admitted, of whom eleven died in the same year.[3] This early version of a nursing home was also a waiting room for death. It was surrounded by fifty acres of land on which the feeble and impoverished were to earn their keep by tending to the vegetables grown there. Inmates could not leave the grounds without permission, and suitable punishments were prescribed for breaking rules, the worst being solitary confinement with bread and water.[4] There is little likelihood that Glover ever suffered such a punishment.

For the next four months no entries relative to Joshua appear in William Montgomery's diary. On the morning of Monday, June 4, 1888, Montgomery had already left to go into town; he was on his way to the Dominion Bank to conduct some business.[5] His wife, Jessie, was just about to leave for the bakery to buy a loaf of bread, when she heard a knock on the door. As she opened it, a messenger from the Great North Western Telegraph Company of Canada held out a folded yellow sheet, the sight of which often caused one's heart to skip a beat. Before she accepted it, she excused herself to get some money for the messenger.[6]

Although Jessie might not ordinarily consider opening communications addressed to her husband, he did have relatives in Dodge County, Wisconsin, and she may have wondered whether someone there had died. Carefully slitting the seal, she unfolded the paper and read, "Joshua Glover is dead. Will you take the body? Answer." It was signed by Jared Irwin, keeper of the Industrial Home, who

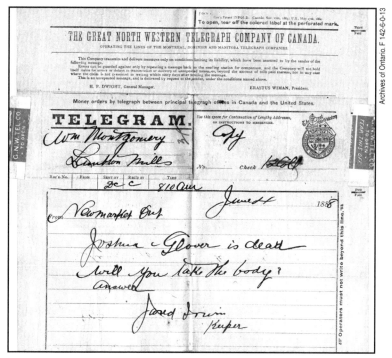

This June 4, 1888, telegram announced the death of Joshua Glover.

had carefully observed the ten-word limitation required to avoid additional charges.[7] The message dated at 8:10 that morning may have led her to believe that Joshua had died in his sleep during the night. In her household accounts book for that date, she penned the entry, "Paid 50 cts for a telegram about Joshes death."[8]

Because Jessie Montgomery was already on her way into town, she probably took the telegram with her, stopped at the bank, and gave it to her husband. The next morning he took the train to Newmarket, once again carefully noting in his daybook the round-trip fare of one dollar and fifty cents.[9] Upon his arrival he learned from the manager that the inspector had taken Josh's body to the medical school at Toronto. The matron at the home told him he could get the body from the school by paying for it.

Arriving in Toronto, Montgomery spoke to a medical student named Cross, who told him that the body had not been delivered there. He then went to the Trinity School of Medicine, and a janitor told him that the body had not arrived there but he would preserve it if it did. He added that if it did eventually arrive there, the longer it stayed, the more it would cost to get it. Montgomery told the janitor he would try to get back there on Thursday. He also spoke to his son Robert, who spoke to Gideon Silverthorne, another student from Etobicoke, who said he would keep a lookout for the body.[10] Having made these efforts to secure a proper burial for Joshua Glover, Montgomery returned home.

It is apparent that William Montgomery had asked to be notified upon Joshua's death so he could arrange for the burial, either next to one of Glover's wives, Ann or Mary Ann, or in a Montgomery plot. However, when he responded to the keeper's telegram within twenty-four hours, he was told that the inspector had made other arrangements.

The keeper, charged with the welfare of the individual inmates, was a person of lesser stature than the inspector, who was the general manager and reported to the common council. One indication of their relative ranks comes from their annual income, $450 for the inspector and a like amount for the keeper and his wife together, she looking after the female inmates.[11]

A number of inmates bequeathed their bodies to the medical school. Obviously, Glover had not done that. Perhaps it was just a mix-up in communication. However, the information given to Montgomery at both the Industrial Home and the medical school about paying for the body made it appear as if the latter institution paid for the bodies their students used and expected repayment if they released one. It is, of course, possible that someone at the home unofficially supplemented his or her income by selling the remains of the indigent and the unclaimed to the school. Such practices were not unheard of in the nineteenth century.

It may be safely assumed that Joshua Glover's last job was to serve as an anatomy lesson for a group of medical students, who would have had the opportunity to examine an elderly man who, according to the death certificate, had died from "congestion of the lungs." The certificate also indicated that he was eighty-one.[12]

Although Joshua Glover never got the gravestone William Montgomery likely would have provided for him, neither does he lie in an unmarked grave. On the grounds of Toronto's St. James Cemetery, the University of Toronto faculty of medicine has placed a headstone inscribed, "Here lie the remains of those who in the interests of others donated their bodies to health education and research. The University of Toronto deeply appreciates their generosity and marks this place to honor their memory."[13]

Benammi Stone Garland, who first came into Joshua's view near those St. Louis courthouse steps in 1850, began life as a member of a privileged family of slave owners, becoming one himself. He and those seeking to preserve and expand slavery did not succeed.

Joshua Glover began life in slavery. He and those of like mind seeking to end the peculiar institution of slavery did succeed. The walls *did* come tumblin' down.

> Joshua Glover
> Freedom Found
> May 1852–June 1888

13

Aftermath

The order of presentation of the characters in these vignettes was determined by the chronology of their appearance in the life of Joshua Glover.

BENAMMI STONE GARLAND   Following the conclusion of his affairs with Sherman Booth, Benammi Garland moved to a farm in St. Charles County, Missouri, where he had reduced holdings and fewer slaves. By 1870 he had moved yet again within that county. By that time he, of course, no longer had slaves, but he did have a hired farmhand and a female house servant. His eldest son, Joseph Parker Garland, one of three selected for cross-interrogatories by Booth's defense, but who did not respond, served in the Confederate Army, following which he moved to Texas, where he became a well-known entertainment impresario. Benammi Garland eventually returned to his sister's home on Garland Hill in Lynchburg, Virginia, where he entered the real estate business. He died there September 6, 1882, his wife following him a few years later.[1]

JUSTINIAN CARTWRIGHT   After he arrived in Racine in 1847, he not only taught his trade of blacksmithing to two of his sons, but one, Finis, became a partner and superintendent in the Racine Wagon and Carriage Company. When the senior Cartwright's first wife, Lucinda, who was white, died, he married another white woman, Jane. This nineteenth-century behavior of quickly remarrying following the death of a wife was not unusual among men with large families, and Cartwright undoubtedly needed help in raising his children. He had at least two other children by his second wife.[2]

In 1861, he had inserted in a local paper the following ad: "a colored man, over 60 years of age, offers to any man who will go to war as a substitute for him $200, to be deposited in a bank, subject to his order on return from service."[3]

A little more than a year and a half later, Cartwright died under tragic circumstances. In November of 1862, there occurred in Racine several fights between white people and colored men, in which the colored men "had been cruelly beaten and almost killed." It is not known if these were connected in any way to similar events happening in other parts of the country, related to the military draft, but shortly after these fights, "the house of Mr. Cartwright was assailed by 4 men, who attempted to break in the front door." Cartwright ran out the rear door, in his bare feet, to get help from his neighbors. As a result of this exposure, he fell ill and shortly thereafter died from "inflamation [sic] of the kidneys and bladder."[4]

DUNCAN SINCLAIR A little more than three years after Glover's capture, Sinclair and his partner, Charles Rice, erected a large sawmill at the village of Tepecotah, Minnesota. Shortly before moving there, while attempting to board a train at Mazomanie, Wisconsin, he slipped, and his foot was crushed between the wheels and the track, requiring amputation. Less than two years after his arrival in Minnesota, his mill burned to the ground. In a letter to Sinclair, a witness to the fire wrote that he believed the fire was deliberate and that everything was destroyed. On April 22, 1888, Sinclair died at age eighty-two in Oak Park, Illinois. He is buried in Racine's Mound Cemetery, which was named after the Native American burial mounds that were in the area before the arrival of the white settlers.[5]

WILLIAM ALBY The third person in Glover's cabin on the night of his capture, Alby may not have disappeared from view as completely as did Nelson Turner, his companion that fateful night. In the 1860 Racine census, there is a William Elba, designated black in the column for color.[6] At that time he was listed as thirty-nine; born in Pennsylvania; having a wife, Rachel, thirty-seven, born in Virginia; and having three sons, William, eleven, Edward, eight, and Travers, one, the two elder born in Missouri and the youngest in Wisconsin. Assuming the accuracy of the data regarding the children, the senior Elba was living in Missouri in 1849 and at least until the birth of his second child in 1852. Although the last name is spelled differently from Glover's card-playing friend, it is known to be relatively common for family names to be misspelled by census enumerators, particularly when the regional accent of the person being counted is different from the enumerator. It may also be that the name was misspelled in the newspaper article in which he was named. If Alby was illiterate, he may not have known how to spell his name.

BYRON PAINE Born in Painesville, Ohio, in 1827, Paine moved to Wisconsin with his father, James Hortensius Paine, a lawyer, at the age of twenty. The move was necessary because his father had been forced to leave his law practice as a result of diminished business associated with his outspoken abolitionist views. When the younger Paine took up the case of Sherman Booth, he had been practicing law for three years. His assertion that the Fugitive Slave Act violated the sovereignty of the northern states, was upheld by the Wisconsin Supreme Court, marking the first successful defense of the doctrine of nullification. He was elected to the Wisconsin Supreme Court in 1859, from which he resigned in 1864 to become a lieutenant colonel in the army, where he served with distinction in Tennessee.[7]

In 1865, following his return to practice, he once again became involved in a case regarding the denial of civil rights to blacks by representing Ezekiel Gillespie, who had been refused the right to vote in Milwaukee. He prevailed through the supreme court, where the right of black suffrage was sustained. In 1867, he was reappointed to the supreme court, where he served until his death in his early forties from erysipelas on January 13, 1871.[8]

JOHN RYCRAFT After being convicted of violating the Fugitive Slave Law, Rycraft remained bitter, claiming that several Milwaukee Democrats had sworn falsely about the extent of his involvement in Glover's escape. In a newspaper interview in 1897 at age seventy-seven, he maintained that George Bingham, C. F. Foote, Charles Watkins, and Edwin Palmer were the primary figures at the break-in of the jail and that George Mallory had lied when he swore he had seen him chopping down the jail door with an ax. He said that he could name several other Democrats who had lied about him and that his arrest and conviction in Milwaukee cost him several thousand dollars and ruined his business as a contractor.

Rycraft explained his interest in abolition as arising from his observation of the treatment of slaves in Nashville, Tennessee, where he had lived as a young man. He was convinced of the evils of slavery by his belief that planters were selling their own children. He was sufficiently upset by seeing outspoken opponents of slavery gunned down in the street, that he disposed of the two slaves he owned before heading for Milwaukee, telling his neighbors that he was moving farther south.[9]

SHERMAN BOOTH   He was initially financially ruined by the civil and criminal trials he endured; it has been estimated that he spent thirty-five thousand dollars on his defense. In addition, his printing presses were seized by Garland to satisfy judgments. In 1859 Booth was accused of seducing a fourteen-year-old girl who occasionally looked after his children. The trial resulted in a hung jury. His other involvement with the law, in regard to the Glover case, continued until early 1861. All these troubles notwithstanding, he managed to publish a weekly newspaper during the war. His wife left him, and he remarried and moved to Chicago, then to Philadelphia, and back to Chicago, where, among other jobs, he was U.S. deputy collector of internal revenue and also made and sold fireplace grates. Eventually he was reunited with his children, from whom he had been estranged for many years. On August 10, 1904, he died in Chicago a few weeks before he would have turned ninety-two.[10]

RICHARD ELA   His difficult life notwithstanding, this Rochester conductor on the UGRR eventually became a town supervisor and chairman of the town board. He also became the largest landowner in the township as well as the owner of considerable land in adjoining counties. His descendants still reside in the town and can point to the spot where a remnant of the plank road, which Olin and Glover took to Racine, is still visible.[11]

ANDREW G. MILLER   In 1873, Judge Miller visited the former Waukesha home of Winchell D. Bacon, by then a hotel, where Glover spent the first night after his rescue from jail. He was in the company of Salmon P. Chase, noted abolitionist attorney. He admitted during that visit that twenty years had modified his opinion of slaveholding and slave hunting and that men's loyalty to party was often stronger than their love for the right.[12]

At about that time Miller also retired from the bench as the longest-serving jurist in the Federal District Court of Wisconsin. He died September 30, 1874. In the eulogy by Edward G. Ryan, then chief justice of the Wisconsin Supreme Court, who had prosecuted Sherman Booth, Ryan said, among other comments: "Judge Miller's intellect was less remarkable than his character. It had nothing brilliant or attractive in it. Its quality was sagacious, not profound; deliberate, not quick; it was respectable rather than remarkable, and was always subordinate to his character. . . . Think as men may of his administration, there was something grand in the lonely self reliance and steadfastness of the man that none can fail to admire . . . he appeared to others arbitrary, when he was only true to his own sense of the dignity and duty of his office."[13]

A. P. DUTTON   After there was no longer a need for his services as a conductor on the UGRR, Dutton remained active in his business, in community affairs, and in racing horses. In the waning years of his life, the city appointed him humane commissioner, a job looking after the welfare of women and children. In addition to the appointment being a sign of respect for his attainments, it was probably also given to him because of his forthright manner and the fact that he and his wife had eleven children. By this time in his life, he was held in high regard in the community and was known as Squire Dutton.[14]

As humane commissioner, Dutton was asked one day to assist a woman who wanted a divorce from her husband. When Dutton saw that her face was black and blue and that she had been kicked in her side, he swore out a warrant for the arrest of the husband. Dutton prosecuted the case in municipal court, and the husband was fined five dollars and costs or thirty days in jail. The wife was willing but unable to pay the fine, and off to jail went the culprit. Shortly thereafter, while out for a walk, Dutton spotted an unattended infant in a baby carriage outside a store, while the mother was shopping within. He located the mother and lectured her about the proper care of babies. A late-nineteenth-century biographical sketch described him as a man whom "nature endowed with strong combativeness, and during the greater part of his life he took no special pains to curb it."[15]

When Dutton died at the age of seventy-nine, on October 31, 1901, the local paper contained a laudatory obituary. It told of his birth in New York in 1822, his arrival as a young man in Racine, and his career as a community leader and a businessman. It related in some detail his ownership of three warehouses and four ships and his success as a grain merchant and freight forwarder on the Great Lakes. Perhaps the most remarkable thing about his obituary was what was not there. There was no mention of his other maritime career, that of a forwarder of fugitive slaves to Canada. Though he died fewer than fifty years after his efforts on behalf of the enslaved, it appeared as though a veil of silence had been draped over that part of his life.[16]

WILLIAM MONTGOMERY   At the time of the death of Joshua Glover, both William Montgomery and his wife, Jessie, were in their mid-fifties. They continued to prosper and eventually moved to Toronto. In late summer of 1915, Jessie suffered a fall, breaking her thigh. Nine weeks later, after contracting pneumonia, she died on October 4, 1915, one year short of fifty years of marriage. She was attended to during her last days by Dr. G. Silverthorne, who at the time of Glover's death was the medical student whom William had asked to be on the lookout for Glover's body.[17]

Jessie Montgomery's detailed obituary reported that of her eight surviving children, many of whom were barristers and physicians, only one, a daughter, was unable to attend the funeral. She was in England with her husband, a lieutenant colonel, commanding the Victoria Rifles. William survived another five years, dying in August 1920 at the age of ninety.[18] Other than a brief notice in the *Toronto Globe*, there was no obituary for this well-known businessman and member of one of the area's pioneer families, probably because no local relative was left to mourn him.

Dedicated June 7, 2003

NATIONAL
UNDERGROUND RAILROAD
NETWORK TO FREEDOM

JOSHUA GLOVER
COMMEMORATIVE MARKER

HAYMARKET SQUARE. On March 10, 1854, the largest crowd that had ever assembled here met to protest the capture of JOSHUA GLOVER, a fugitive slave who had lived and worked in Racine for two years. A committee of 100 then took a boat to Milwaukee where Glover had been jailed. They aided in his rescue and subsequent journey on the Underground Railroad. He eventually escaped by ship to Canada, where he lived in freedom until his death, June 8, 1888.

This marker commemorates Glover and the citizens of Racine who, at their peril, aided one of their own out of the bondage of slavery.

Placed by the LINKS, Incorporated, Greater Racine Chapter, and Racine Heritage Museum

RACINE
HERITAGE
MUSEUM

THE LINKS, INC.

This commemorative marker was installed in Racine, Wisconsin, in June 2003. A larger monument to Joshua Glover is planned for Cathedral Square in downtown Milwaukee. Both sites will be recognized on the National Park Service's Underground Railroad Network to Freedom.

The Search for Joshua Glover

While this book is the result of the efforts of the two whose names are on the title page, no book comes to print as the result of the efforts exclusively of the authors. Our search began about a decade ago when Ruby West Jackson was rooting through the archives of Racine Heritage Museum researching material for *Heritage Wisconsin*, a booklet to be published by the Wisconsin Department of Tourism showcasing African American history in the state. It was there she discovered Joshua Glover, a runaway slave whose capture by his owner more than 150 years ago initiated a series of events that had local, regional, and national consequences, as well as eventually leading Glover to many years of freedom in Canada.

Jackson was already familiar with the scarcity of written material about black history in general, and fugitive slaves in particular, and knew it would be difficult to flesh out the story of one illiterate man who had committed the illegal act of stealing himself from his owner. The first confirmation that the story of Joshua Glover was no exception occurred when she discovered that all previously written accounts of Glover's role in the matter ended with some variation of the phrase ". . . and he escaped to Canada." This would then be followed by careful analysis of the political effects of "the Glover affair" on Wisconsin as well as the country as a whole.

As Jackson was telling Walter T. McDonald about some of her discoveries and the difficulties she was having finding sufficient material to enhance the story, she sensed his interest and asked the fateful question, "Mac, why don't we write a book about this?"

On that day in the mid-1990s, an unlikely partnership was formed between two friends, one the Milledgeville, Georgia-raised great-granddaughter of slaves, who had been an educator for more than five decades, and the other, a Brooklyn, New York-raised great-grandson of Irish peasants under British rule, who was mostly retired from a five-decade career as a clinical and forensic psychologist.

Mac's reply to that question launched us on an odyssey that included two countries, five states, and more than a baker's dozen of cities, towns, and villages. Our first trip to Canada, seeking information on that terminus of the UGRR as well as evidence of Glover's presence there, was marked by equal portions of enthusiasm and naïveté and resulted in a mixed bag. Windsor produced much evidence about Caroline Quarles, also a subject of Ruby's interest. Quarles is believed to be the first documented slave to come through Wisconsin, arriving there about 1842 after escaping from her owner in St. Louis. We found nothing on Joshua Glover. The Walls Museum and the Dresden Museum also yielded naught. Returning to Racine, somewhat disappointed, Mac got the bright idea of searching for Glover in the 1871 Ontario Census Index. Bingo! There he was, living in Etobicoke, now a suburb of Toronto. A call to the public library there yielded the name of a woman who was interested in black history and also worked as a docent at Montgomery's Inn, a living museum of nineteenth-century local history. A call to her at the museum met with some delay, as she was baking bread. When she came to the phone, Mac asked whether the name Joshua Glover meant anything to her. He was rewarded with a scream of recognition. Not only had she heard of him, but he had been employed by the original owner of the inn.

Within weeks, we were in Canada again, this time Toronto, where Hilary Dawson led us to treasure troves of information about Glover and the lives of other former slaves who had escaped to Canada. Her efforts and her prodigious ability to unearth events concerning Glover were of enormous help in writing this book. Additionally, her proofreading skills prevented such gauche American mistakes as lowercasing "Crown," while her previously unrecognized teleportation ability caused an unpublished memoir written by an obscure minister, and containing references to Glover, to fall at her feet as she was passing a bookshelf at the inn. After we returned to our homes, she continued to provide us with additional material we requested, as well as other information she felt would be useful. We are forever grateful to her.

In our search for Joshua Glover the person, we encountered a problem, although not an unusual one when engaged in slavery research. He could neither read nor write. The number of spoken words attributed to him was fewer than fifty. We found no accounts of any moods, thoughts, or states of mind attributed to him, other than the few utterances described.

Because there was no question that Glover was a sentient human being, capable of a wide range of moods and feelings, and because it was quite likely he would respond to a variety of situations in ways similar to others under similar circumstances, we thought it appropriate to describe his likely feelings and moods at certain critical points in his life. These attributions are followed by endnotes—citations to a variety of published accounts of the testimony of former slaves regarding their fears and apprehensions in similar situations. In addition, the authors relied on their combined knowledge base regarding the responses of other human beings to stressful situations.

There remains only one other person to mention in connection with our search. When we began the journey that culminated in this book, we were determined that its title character should be its central focus. As with the vast majority of fugitive slaves, the records of his words and deeds came from others whose primary concerns were "larger" ones such as emancipation vs. slavery, secession vs. Union, publishing newsworthy items, and showcasing the virtues and vices of their respective supporters and opponents. We painstakingly teased out Glover's story from the vast amount of print devoted to these other subjects. In addition to our own determination, there was one other important factor, which should more appropriately be called a force. His name is Joshua Glover.

When we began this project more than a decade ago, we thought we were in control of the rate at which we worked, the incidents we chose to emphasize, and those we chose to minimize or ignore. After all, it was our idea to write this book, wasn't it? That may be so. But true or not in the beginning, we were inexorably taken over by Joshua himself. Yes, we *can* call him by his first name. After all, that's what he did to us when he awakened us, at times simultaneously, in the middle of the night, even though our individual homes are more than a hundred miles distant from one another.

Joshua also had another trick he used when he wanted to call our attention to something important that he believed we had overlooked. Regardless of whether we were eating dinner, talking to a friend, or simply reading a newspaper or watching television, he distracted us from what we were doing with a request that we add, subtract, or otherwise modify some word, sentence, or passage to more clearly reflect its importance here and now. To those we might have been speaking to at the time: you were not boring us, and we were not being boors. We were once again taken over by Joshua, who would brook no opposition to the righteous telling of his story.

Perhaps now that this book is published and in circulation, Joshua will leave us in peace. We believe, however, that some readers may have had similar experiences while reading or after finishing the book. If this has happened to you, don't be frightened. Joshua has simply found his way into your heart, as he has done with us and with the hearts of many of those who knew him a century and a half before we did. This phenomenon may cause you occasional interrupted sleep or may put a dull glaze across your eyes when you are talking to someone or otherwise cause you to behave in slightly peculiar ways. We assume no responsibility for these aberrations, and no refunds will be given.

Notes

Abbreviations of Frequent Sources

AO — Archives of Ontario
LB — Toronto Metropolitan Reference Library, Baldwin Room
MD — *Milwaukee Free Democrat*
MS — *Milwaukee Sentinel*
NARA — National Archives and Research Administration, Great Lakes Region
PF — *Provincial Freeman*
RA — *Racine Advocate*
RHM — Racine Heritage Museum
TG — *Toronto Globe*

Chapter 1

1. NARA. Records of District Courts, Eastern District of Wisconsin, Milwaukee. Law Records 1848–1862. Affidavit of B. S. Garland, March 9, 1854.
2. Frederick Bancroft, *Slave Trading in the Old South* (Columbia, SC: University of South Carolina Press, 1996), 141.
3. Ibid., 142.
4. Ibid., 144.
5. Harrison A. Trexler, *Slavery in Missouri 1804–1865* (Baltimore: The Johns Hopkins Press, 1914), 49–50.
6. Bancroft, *Slave Trading*, 146.
7. Ibid., 91.
8. Trexler, *Slavery in Missouri*, 31–32.
9. John W. Blassingame, ed., *Slave Testimony* (Baton Rouge, LA: Louisiana State University Press, 1977), 504.
10. NARA. Records of District Courts. Response to interrogatories.

11. In "The Public Life and Private Affairs of Sherman M. Booth," *Wisconsin Magazine of History* 82, no. 3 (Spring 1999): 167–197, Diane Butler states her belief that "Benami" is the proper spelling of Garland's first name. Our sources include ten examples of his name, six of which are rendered as "Benammi." The remaining four are Benoni, Benjamin, Bennami, and B. S. Garland. Chronologically, they are St. Louis Circuit Court Records, re: Estate of Sanford "Benoni"; ibid., April term, 1849, "Benammi"; ibid., September 5, 1849, "Benammi"; Federal District Court, Wisconsin, March 9, 1854, Affidavit of Benammi S. Garland, signed, "B. S. Garland"; Wisconsin Supreme Court, June term, 1854, p. 15, "Benammi"; Federal Court, Eastern District of Wisconsin, January term, 1855, Motion to quash indictment, "Benammi"; Federal Court, Wisconsin, Indictment, January 1855, "Benammi"; Missouri Supreme Court, October term, 1857. The final two syllables of "Benjamin" are crossed out and replaced with, "ammie," which is written above.

He often signed his name as "B. S. Garland." He named his first-born child "Benjamin." Garland himself was named after his maternal grandfather, Benammi Stone. It is likely that he did not particularly like the spelling of his given name. He was informally known as "Ben." Based on this data, the authors' conclusion is that "Benammi" is the preferred spelling of his name.

12. Blassingame, *Slave Testimony*, 507.

13. Glover's recitation of abilities is supplied from an available list of tasks he performed when employed in Canada. Ibid., 503.

14. *Missouri Republican*, May 19, 1852.

15. The total number of words recorded as having been spoken by Joshua Glover is fewer than one hundred. In order to render him as a sentient human being with thoughts and feelings similar to others in bondage, it was necessary to ascribe certain thoughts to him in our narrative. We have appended here sixteen citations of first-person slave narratives from four sources, generally regarded as having high reliability. They are divided into two groups:

Fears of being sold south: Bancroft, *Slave Trading*, 47–48, 90–91, 138–139, 289–290; Blassingame, *Slave Testimony*,

108, 221–222, 504, 506, 518, 697, 700; Gary Collison, *Shadrach Minkins. From Fugitive Slave to Citizen* (Cambridge, MA: Harvard University Press, 1997), 107.

Fears of punishments for infractions or running: Blassingame, *Slave Testimony*, 218, 276–277, 501–502; Herbert G. Gutman, *The Black Family in Slavery and Freedom 1750–1925* (New York: Vintage Books a Division of Random House, 1976), 148.

16. Blassingame, *Slave Testimony*, 502.
17. Ibid., xliv, quoting Samuel G. Howe, *The Refugees from Slavery in Canada West* (Boston: unknown publisher, 1864), 3.
18. Trexler, *Slavery in Missouri*, 179–181.
19. NARA. Records of District Courts. Affidavit.
20. Seventh Federal Census, 1850, St. Louis County. Agriculture Schedule.
21. Ibid., Slave Schedule.
22. Ibid., Agriculture Schedule.
23. St. Louis County, Circuit Court Records, 1845 et. seq.
24. *Garland v. LeBeau*, St. Louis County, Probate Court Records, 1859.
25. Missouri State Archives, "Missouri's Dred Scott Case, 1846–1857," http://www.sos.mo.gov/archives/resources/africanamericans/scott/scott.asp (accessed May 15, 2006).
26. *Garland v. LeBeau.*
27. Trexler, *Slavery in Missouri*, 185.
28. Ibid.
29. Blassingame, *Slave Testimony*, 401–410.
30. Trexler, *Slavery in Missouri*, 57–59.
31. Ibid., 113.
32. Amherst Circuit Court Deed Book, Book X, May 10, 1839, 79.

Chapter 2

1. "Africans in America, the Terrible Transformation. Part 1: Virginia Recognizes Slavery," http://pbs.org/wgbh/aia/part1/1narr3.html (accessed May 15, 2006).
2. Missouri Compromise, 1820.

3. Larry Gara, *The Liberty Line* (Lexington, KY: University of Kentucky Press, 1961; repr. with new preface, 1996), 192–193.
4. Gara, *Liberty Line*, xii.
5. *PF*, August 19, 1854.
6. *New York Times Magazine*, February 13, 2001, 53 et seq.

Chapter 3

1. *History of Waukesha County* (Chicago, Western Historical Company, 1880), 458–464.
2. *Burlington, Wisconsin: The First 150 Years 1835–1990* (Burlington, WI: Burlington Historical Society, 1991), 19.
3. *MS*, October 10, 1850.
4. Milwaukee Census, 1850.
5. Milwaukee City Directory, 1854.
6. *MS*, October 10, 1850.
7. Milwaukee Public Museum, Watson File.
8. *MS*, October 10, 1850.
9. Milwaukee Public Museum, Watson File.
10. *MS*, October 10, 1850.

Chapter 4

1. Personal communication between the authors and Eric Robinson, Alton, Illinois, 1999.
2. *MS*, April 1, 1854.
3. Ibid.
4. Federal Census, 1850, St. Louis. Slave Schedule.
5. *MS*, April 1, 1854.

Chapter 5

1. Francis J. Reich, "A Comprehensive Biography of Gilbert Knapp, the Founder of Racine" (unpublished manuscript, Racine Public Library, 1976), 1–3.
2. Ibid.

3. *Racine Journal Times*, September 9, 1997.
4. Reich, "Biography of Gilbert Knapp," 7.
5. Racine City Directory, 1850.
6. Susan Payne, "Memoir" (unpublished manuscript, RHM, ca. 1930).
7. Racine City Directory, 1850.
8. U.S. Census, Racine, 1850.
9. U.S. Census, Racine, 1860.
10. Ibid.
11. *Racine Weekly Journal*, December 10, 1862.
12. *RA*, March 12, 1854.
13. Frederick Bancroft, *Slave Trading in the Old South* (Columbia, SC: University of South Carolina Press, 1996), 162–163.
14. John G. Gregory, *Southeastern Wisconsin*, vol. 1 (Chicago: S.J. Clarke, 1932), 458.
15. Ibid., 472.
16. Racine City Directory, 1850.
17. Gregory, *Southeastern Wisconsin*, 457.
18. Ibid.
19. U.S. Census, Racine, 1860.

Chapter 6

1. U.S. Census, Racine County, 1850.
2. *RA*, March 12, 1854.
3. *MS*, March 13, 1854.
4. Ibid.
5. *RA*, March 13, 1854; *MS*, March 13, 1854.
6. U.S. Census, Racine County, 1850.
7. *MS*, March 13, 1854.
8. *RA*, March 20, 1854.
9. Ibid., March 12, 1854.
10. Ibid.
11. *MD*, March 11, 1854; *MD*, March, 13, 1854.
12. *RA*, March 25, 1854.
13. Ibid, March 13, 1854
14. Ibid, March 12, 1854.
15. *MS*, April 1, 1854.

16. Anthony J. Von Frank, *The Trials of Anthony Burns: Freedom and Slavery in Emerson's Boston* (Cambridge, MA: Harvard University Press, 1998), 131–132.
17. Ibid., 132.
18. NARA. Records of District Courts, Eastern District of Wisconsin, Milwaukee. Criminal Files 1848–1862. Warrant March 9, 1854; *RA*, March 23, 1854.
19. *MS*, March 13, 1854.
20. *RA*, March 12, 1854; *MS*, March 25, 1854.
21. *RA*, March 25, 1854.
22. *RA*, December 9, 1854.
23. *MS*, March 12, 1854.
24. Diane S. Butler, "The Public Life and Private Affairs of Sherman M. Booth," *Wisconsin Magazine of History* 82, no. 3 (Spring 1999): 167–197.
25. *MD*, March 13, 1854.
26. Handbill printed by Sherman Booth, March 13, 1854, at his newspaper office.
27. *RA*, March 12, 1854.
28. *MD*, March 13, 1854.
29. *RA*, March 25, 1854.
30. James I. Clark, *Wisconsin Defies the Fugitive Slave Law* (Madison, WI: State Historical Society of Wisconsin, 1955), 6.
31. *MS*, March 22, 1854.
32. *MD*, March 13, 1854.
33. *The Evening Wisconsin*, July 19, 1843; *MS*, June 10, 1900; Harry Bolton, ed, *St. John's Cathedral: The First Hundred Years 1847–1947* (Milwaukee: Wetzel Bros., 1947), 31–34; *War Commandery Military Order of the United States*, vol. 4 (Milwaukee: Burdick and Allen, 1914), 221.
34. *MS*, June 10, 1900.
35. Ibid.
36. *RA*, March 12, 1854.
37. *MS*, June 10, 1900.
38. *MS*, March 23, 1854.
39. *RA*, March 12, 1854.
40. *MS*, March 23, 1854.

41. *MS*, April 1, 1854.
42. Ibid.
43. *MS*, March 24, 1854.
44. *MS*, March 13, 1854.

Chapter 7

1. *Memoirs of Waukesha County*, vol. 2 (Madison, WI: Western Historical Association, 1907), 113.
2. U.S. Census, Milwaukee, 1850.
3. *History of Waukesha County* (Chicago: Wisconsin Historical Co., 1880), 459.
4. *History of Waukesha County* (Chicago: Wisconsin Historical Co, 1893), 493.
5. Ibid., 471–472.
6. *Landmark*, Volume 40, #4, Winter, 1997 (Waukesha County History Society).
7. Ibid.
8. Ibid.
9. Willard S. Griswold, "History of First Congregational Church of Waukesha, Wisconsin" (unpublished manuscript, Waukesha County History Museum, January 20, 1908), 11–14.
10. *History of Waukesha County* (Chicago: Wisconsin Historical Co., 1880), 549–550.
11. C. C. Olin, *Early Anti-Slavery Excitement in Wisconsin 1842–1860* (Madison, WI: Wisconsin Historical Society, c. 1880), microfilm 301, reel 1.
12. Ibid.
13. Ibid.
14. U.S. Census, Rochester, WI, 1850.
15. Olin, *Early Anti-Slavery Excitement.*
16. RHM, "Racine's Early Church History."
17. RHM, Genealogy File. M. P. Kinney.
18. *Memoirs of Waukesha County*, 115.
19. John G. Gregory, ed., *Southeastern Wisconsin Old Milwaukee County* (Chicago: S. J. Clarke, 1932), 769.

20. Susan Payne, "Memoir" (unpublished manuscript, RHM, ca. 1933).
21. Ibid.
22. Don Jensen, "Kenosha Kaleidoscope: Images of the Past" (unpublished manuscript, Kenosha History Museum, Date Unknown), 18–21; William C. Bacon (as told by Capt. Theo. Fellows), "A Story of the Underground Railway in Bristol" (unpublished manuscript, Kenosha History Museum, Date Unknown), 39–42.
23. Burlington Historical Society, Underground Railroad file.
24. *Burlington, Wisconsin: The First Hundred Fifty Years. 1835–1990* (Burlington, WI: Burlington Historical Society, 1991), 13.
25. *Southport Telegraph Racine County Wisconsin Territory*, August 18, 1840.
26. Eugene W. Leach, "Racine County Militant" (unpublished manuscript, Racine Public Library, 1915), 31.
27. *Southeastern Wisconsin Old Milwaukee*, 605.
28. Ibid.
29. Sherman Booth to Ida Ela, letter, November 8, 1903, Rochester, WI, Public Library.
30. *Portrait and Biographical Album of Racine and Kenosha Counties* (Chicago: Lake City Publishing Co., 1892), 905–907.
31. RHM, A. P. Dutton Scrapbook, undated newspaper item ca. 1897.
32. Ibid., unsourced newspaper article.
33. Ibid.
34. Unsourced clipping of newspaper advertisement, 1846.
35. *Portrait and Biographical Album*, 906.
36. RHM, Dutton Scrapbook, newspaper item, November 14, 1899.
37. Ibid., undated newspaper item.
38. Wilbur H. Siebert, *The Underground Railroad from Slavery to Freedom* (Gloucester, MA: Peter Smith, 1898), 83.
39. *Milwaukee Journal*, September 3, 1993.
40. *MS*, May 22, 1848.
41. Ibid.
42. *MS*, April 6, 1850.

Chapter 8

1. *MD*, March 13, 1854.
2. *Ableman v. Booth* and *U.S. v. Booth*, 21 Howard 506 (U.S. District Court of Wisconsin, December 1858).
3. NARA. Records of U.S. District Court of Wisconsin. Criminal Case Files 1849–1862.
4. *RA*, March 25, 1854 (quoting *St. Louis Intelligencer* account).
5. NARA. U.S. District Court of Wisconsin. Law Records, 1848–1862; Appearance Docket Books 1849–1862 vol. B.
6. *MS*, December 12, 1854.
7. *MS*, September 12, 1853.
8. *History of Milwaukee* (Chicago: The Western Historical Company. A. T. Andeas, Prop., 1881), 242.
9. *Wisconsin Magazine of History*, December 1947, 182–183.
10. *MS*, August 22, 1849.
11. *MS*, January 10, 1854.
12. *History of Milwaukee, Wisconsin*, 242.
13. Ibid.
14. Ibid.
15. *MS*, April 5, 1854.
16. *MS*, July 10, 1854.
17. *MS*, August 3, 1854.
18. *MS*, August 5, 1854.
19. *MS*, September 2, 1854.
20. NARA. U.S. District Court of Wisconsin. Appearances Docket Book 1849–1862.
21. *History of Milwaukee*, 242.
22. *MS*, April 5, 1854.
23. *MS*, April 6, 1854.
24. NARA. U.S. District Court of Wisconsin. January term, 1855.
25. *MS*, March 22, 1854.
26. NARA. U.S. District Court of Wisconsin. Criminal Case Files 1849–1862.
27. *RA*, July 12, 1854.
28. *RA*, July 14, 1854.
29. NARA. U.S. District Court of Wisconsin. Interrogatories, 1849–1862.

30. Ibid.
31. Ibid.
32. Ibid.
33. *History of Milwaukee*, 245.
34. NARA. U.S. District Court of Wisconsin. Appearance Docket Books.
35. *MD*, February 4, 1855.
36. NARA. U.S. District Court of Wisconsin. Criminal Court Records.
37. Ibid.
38. *MS*, January 16, 1852; August4, 1853; December 9, 1855.
39. *MS*, December 21, 1858.
40. James Bilotta, *Race and the Rise of the Republican Party 1848–1855* (New York: Lang Publishing, 1992), 123.
41. Ibid., 124.
42. *MS*, April 14, 1854.
43. "Little White Schoolhouse," http://www.ripon-wi-com/ripon-wi/page.asp?p+little_white_schoolhouse (accessed May 15, 2006).
44. *Madison State Journal*, July 18, 1854; *MS*, January 16, 1860.
45. *MS*, January 16, 1860.
46. *History of Milwaukee*, 651–652.
47. NARA. President Buchanan's commutation of Booth's sentence, March 2, 1861.

Chapter 9

1. *Owen Sound Comet*, March 31, 1854; *National Advance and County of Simcoe General Advertiser*, March 29, 1854; *Barrie Herald*, March 29, 1854; *PF*, March 25, 1854.
2. LB, Montgomery Documents, 51–53, 68.
3. At the time of Glover's arrival in Canada, the country was in transition from the British pound, shilling, pence method of reckoning to the decimal system, which was finalized in 1858. Thomas Montgomery tended to combine the British system with decimal notation. Later, his son William used the decimal system. In 1854, a Canadian shilling, which was based on the

Halifax currency system, was worth ten pence British and twenty cents U.S.; therefore, five shillings equaled one dollar and one pound equaled four dollars.

4. Typical daily wages in 1854: bricklayers, ten shillings (two dollars); carpenters and tinsmiths, seven shillings (one dollar and forty cents); male tailors, five shillings (one dollar); female tailors, one shilling and three pence (twenty-five cents). Day laborers earned up to five shillings, while girls and boys between twelve and fourteen got about one shilling and six pence (thirty-five cents). Work such as cutting timber, splitting rails, and various agricultural tasks were sometimes paid on a piecework basis.

5. Bev Hykel and Carl Benn, *Thomas Montgomery. Portrait of a Nineteenth Century Businessman*, rev. ed. (1980; repr., Etobicoke, Ontario: Borough of Etobicoke Historical Board, 1996), 9.

6. Ibid.

7. Ibid., 21.

8. Various Authors, *The Villages of Etobicoke* (Etobicoke, Ontario: The Etobicoke Historical Board, undated), 21.

9. *A Walking Tour of the Village of Islington.* (Montgomery's Inn: The Etobicoke Historical Board, undated), 3.

10. Hykel, *Thomas Montgomery*, 22.

11. *A Walking Tour*, 23.

12. Hilary J. Dawson, *Portraits from the Past: A Celebration of Black History Month* (Toronto, CA: Ontario Black History Society, February 1996).

13. Canada West Census, York County, Etobicoke Township, 1851.

14. Canada West Census, 1842. Home District return—aggregate of inhabitants of Etobicoke.

15. Hilary J. Dawson, *Thomas Montgomery's Black Neighbors* (Etobicoke, Ontario: Montgomery's Inn, February 1997).

16. LB, Montgomery Documents, 1838.

17. Hykel, *Thomas Montgomery*, 39.

18. Ibid.

19. Ibid., 40.

20. Ibid., 39.

21. Ibid., 41.
22. LB, Montgomery Documents, 37–39.
23. LB, Montgomery Documents, 44–48, 46.
24. Hykel, *Thomas Montgomery*, 39.
25. Ibid., 42.
26. Ibid., 43.
27. Ibid., 45.
28. Ibid., 52.
29. Ibid., 52–54.
30. Ibid., 69.
31. Ibid., 72.
32. Ibid.
33. Ibid., 75.
34. Ibid., 77.
35. Ibid., 79.
36. Ibid., 77.
37. Ibid., 78.
38. Ibid., 82.
39. Robin W. Winks, *The Blacks in Canada, a History*, 2nd ed. (Montreal: McGill-Queen's University Press, 1997), 111.
40. Ibid., 169.
41. Ibid., 172.
42. Ibid., 174.
43. Ibid., 174–175.
44. Ibid., 31–32.
45. Ibid., 115.
46. Ibid., 212–213. Also, *Social Conditions Among Negroes in Upper Canada Before 1865*, vol. 22 (Ontario: Ontario Historical Society, 1925), 147.
47. James W. St. G. Walker, *Racial Discrimination in Canada: The Black Experience*, Historical Booklet no. 41 (Ottawa, ON: Canadian Historical Association, 1985), 11.
48. Winks, *Blacks in Canada*, 246–247.
49. Daniel G. Hill, "Negroes in Toronto 1793–1865," http://www.qesnrecit.qc.ca/mpages/unit4/u4p74.htm (accessed May 30, 2006).

Chapter 10

1. Hilary J. Dawson, *The Black Heritage of Etobicoke's Communities* (Etobicoke, Ontario: Montgomery's Inn, February 1998).
2. Hilary J. Dawson, *Thomas Montgomery's Black Neighbors* (Etobicoke, Ontario: Montgomery's Inn, February 1997).
3. LB, Thomas Montgomery Documents, 56–94.
4. Ibid.
5. Ibid., 24, 25.
6. Thomas Montgomery's Notebook, AO, F-142–8-0–9.
7. *TG*, October 1, 1858.
8. *TG*, October 2, 1858.
9. *TG*, September 29, 1858.
10. *TG*, October 2, 1858.
11. *TG*, October 1, 1858.
12. LB, Thomas Montgomery Documents, 56–94, 67–68.
13. Ibid.
14. Ontario Census, Township of Etobicoke, 1861.
15. *RA*, December 9, 1854.
16. Ontario Census, Township of Etobicoke, 1861.
17. Hilary J. Dawson, *Portraits from the Past: A Celebration of Black History Month* (Etobicoke, Ontario: Montgomery Inn, February 1996).
18. James W. St. G. Walker, *Racial Discrimination in Canada: The Black Experience*, Historical Booklet no. 41 (Ottawa, Ontario: Canadian Historical Association, Date Unknown), 10, 11.
19. LB, Thomas Montgomery Documents, 56–94, 139.
20. Ibid., 143, 144.
21. Ibid., 161, 162.
22. Ontario Census, Township of Etobicoke, 1871.
23. Death Certificate #033437, AO, MS 935 R4.
24. LB, Thomas Montgomery Documents, 56–94, 176, 177; Toronto Diocesan Archives, St. George's Islington Burial Registration, 1872.
25. LB, Thomas Montgomery Documents, 56–94, 180–183.
26. Township of Etobicoke Assessment Rolls, 1874.
27. LB, Thomas Montgomery Documents, 56–94, 187, 188.

28. Ibid., 188, 189.
29. Ibid., 191, 192.
30. Ibid.
31. Ibid.
32. Bev Hykel and Carl Benn, *Thomas Montgomery. Portrait of a Nineteenth Century Businessman*, rev. ed. (1980; repr., Montgomery's Inn, Borough of Etobicoke Historical Board, 1996), 19.
33. LB, Thomas Montgomery Documents, 56–94, 198, 199.
34. Death Registrations 1869–1927, *MS* 935 R30.
35. LB, Thomas Montgomery Documents, 56–94, 206.
36. The Reverend G. Moore Morgan, *Memoirs of a Parson 1959* (unpublished manuscript retrieved from trash August 1, 1983, by staff of Montgomery's Inn).

Chapter 11

1. *TG*, May 24, 1884.
2. "Serious Stabbing Affray," *TG*, May 26, 1884.
3. AO, Judges' Bench Books, Cameron: Criminal Assizes, March 1884–April 1885.
4. "Serious Stabbing Affray," *TG*, May 26, 1884.
5. AO, City of Toronto, Gaol Descriptive Book, 1884.
6. AO, Minute Book of William Montgomery, May 24, 1884.
7. Ibid., May 26, 1884.
8. York County Atlas, AO, 1878.
9. AO, Diary of William Montgomery, June 25, 1884.
10. Bev Hykel and Carl Benn, *Thomas Montgomery. Portrait of a Nineteenth Century Businessman*, rev. ed. (1980; repr., Montgomery's Inn, Borough of Etobicoke Historical Board, 1996), 76.
11. AO, Criminal Indictment Case Files, Joshua Glover, 1884.
12. AO, Toronto Gaol: Prisoners' Effects, 1883–86.
13. AO, Minute Book of William Montgomery, May 28, 1884.
14. "Police News," *TG*, May 26, 1884.
15. "After the Holiday," *The Evening Telegram*, May 26, 1884.
16. "Serious Stabbing Affray," *TG*, May 26, 1884.
17. AO, Minute Book of William Montgomery, June 13, 1884.
18. AO, Judges' Bench Books, Cameron: Criminal Assizes, March 1884–April 1885.

19. Criminal Indictment Case Files, Deposition of Mary Butler; AO, Judges' Bench Books, Cameron: Criminal Assizes, March 1884–April 1885.
20. Ibid.
21. AO, Criminal Assize Clerk Reports, 1882–85, York County, Summer 1884.
22. Ibid.
23. AO, Minute Book of William Montgomery, July 23, 1884.
24. AO, Diary of William Montgomery, September 19, 1884.
25. AO, Ontario Central Prison Register, 6483–6535.

Chapter 12

1. AO, Montgomery Family Papers, F-142–7-0–6, January 30, 1888.
2. Ibid., January 31, 1888.
3. "The Industrial Home, Newmarket," *Families* 26, no. 4 (1987): 225–226.
4. Ibid, 226.
5. AO, Montgomery Family Papers, F-142–6-0–13, June 4, 1888.
6. Ibid., F-142–6-0–14, June 4, 1888.
7. Ibid., F-142–6-0–13, June 4, 1888.
8. Ibid., F-143–6-0–14, June 4, 1888.
9. Ibid., F-142–7-0–13, June 5, 1888.
10. Ibid.
11. *Newmarket Intelligencer and Advertiser*, June 14, 1895.
12. AO, Death Certificate MS935 R52 Reg. No. 020546, June 3, 1888.
13. AO, Plat Map, St. James Cemetery, Toronto, Canada.

Chapter 13

1. U.S. Census, St. Charles County, St. Charles Township, Missouri, 1860; U.S. Census, St. Charles County, Dardennes Township, Missouri, 1870; *A Memorial and Biographical History of McLennan, Falls, Bell and Coryell Counties, Texas*

(Chicago: Lewis Publishing Co., 1893), 649–650; *The Lynchburg Virginian*, September 7, 1882, 3 and June 8, 1885, 1; U.S. Census, Racine, Wisconsin, 1850.

2. U.S. Census, Racine, Wisconsin, 1860.
3. *Racine Daily Journal*, April 24, 1861.
4. *Racine Weekly Journal*, December 10, 1862.
5. *Racine Daily Journal*, September 1, 1857; *Racine Democrat*, September 14, 1857; *Racine Weekly Advocate*, August 3, 1859; *Racine Daily Journal*, July 29, 1859; *Racine Daily Journal*, April 24, 1888.
6. U.S. Census, Racine, Wisconsin, 1860.
7. Legislative Proceedings, 27 Wis. (Supreme Court of Wisconsin, January 17, 1870), 26; ibid., 23.
8. *Gillespie v. Palmer* 20 WIS 544 (1866); Legislative Proceedings, 27 Wis. (Supreme Court of Wisconsin, January 17, 1870), 24.
9. *MS*, August 1, 1897.
10. Booth and Coors family papers, 1818–1908, Milwaukee Manuscript Collection, BB Golda Meir Library, University of Wisconsin Library; Diane S. Butler, "The Public Life and Private Affairs of Sherman M. Booth," *Wisconsin Magazine of History* 82, no. 3 (Spring 1999): 167–197.
11. Personal communication between authors and Ela family, 1997.
12. Leach, 34.
13. Legislative Proceedings (Wisconsin Supreme Court, January term, 1875), 26.
14. RHM, A. P. Dutton Scrapbook; *Racine Times*, June 13, 1896.
15. RHM, A. P. Dutton Scrapbook; *Portrait and Biographical Album of Racine and Kenosha Counties* (Chicago: Lake City Publishing Co., 1892), 905.
16. *Racine Daily Journal*, October 31, 1901.
17. *Toronto Star*, October 16, 1915; Toronto Death Register, 1915; AO, Montgomery Family Papers, F-142–7-0–6, January 30, 1888.
18. *Toronto Star*, October 16, 1915; *TG*, August 23, 1920.

Index

Page numbers in italics indicate illustrations.